en, Wo

Women, Work, and Volunteering

HERTA LOESER

ILLUSTRATIONS BY INGE PAVLOWSKY

Beacon Press *Boston*

To my husband, Hans Loeser

> for his infinite patience, his love, his support, and his rare good judgment. His standards of excellence and trenchant criticism – potentially devastating, had they not gone together with his ultimate confidence in me – caused me to try my best.

Copyright © 1974 by Herta Loeser
Beacon Press books are published under the auspices of the Unitarian Universalist Association
First published as a Beacon Paperback in 1975
Printed in the United States of America

9 8 7 6 5 4 3 2

Library of Congress Cataloging in Publication Data

Loeser, Herta.
  Women, work, and volunteering.
  1. Women volunteers in social service — United States.   I. Title.
HV91.L62   361.6   74-209
ISBN 0-8070-0878-8
ISBN 0-8070-0879-6 (pbk.)

Contents

v

PART THREE

Practical Resources

Appendixes

Preface

This book is meant as a practical aid for American women, particularly those living in cities and suburbs, to help them decide whether they should do volunteer work, and if so how to get started. It should help them think through what kind of work they can and should do and whether they should look on their volunteer jobs as a temporary or a permanent part of their lives.

A practical aid, yes! But no book on volunteering for women published in the 1970s can be truly practical, if it does not first tackle these initial questions: Does volunteering still make sense for American women today, or is it counterproductive to social change, to governmental responsibility, to women's aspirations? And what goals, indeed what dreams, for the future justify voluntarism as a continuing American institution?

Part One deals with these issues. The discussion concludes that, far from having to be discarded as a precondition to women's liberation and a more just world, volunteering can and should be an essential element of both women's *and men's* future lifestyles.

The structure of voluntarism in America was built largely by women over the last 100 to 150 years. Though it is in the midst of profound and needed changes at this very moment, it is still a valid avenue for women's pioneering contributions to the world of tomorrow.

The modern women of and for whom I write range from teenage to old age. Vast differences in age and life experiences notwithstanding, their goals and achievements as volunteers have, surprisingly, much in common. But my experience also leaves no doubt, particularly when it comes to practical advice of the *how*, *when*, and *where* variety, that these women's abilities and needs differ so greatly that only advice tailored to the specific life stage of the individual is truly practical and helpful. Indeed, age may not be the most crucial differentiator. A retired bookkeeper may, when seeking volunteer counseling, have more in common with a high school drop-out than a forty-year-old married woman has with a forty-year-old widow or divorced woman.

Part Two of this book, therefore, deals specifically with how a woman at any of several stages in life, or faced with particular circumstances, can decide whether volunteering is for her and how to translate an affirmative answer into a satisfying, productive volunteer activity, either as a bridge to something else or as a permanent part of her life. If a woman is in the questioning stage of her decision to volunteer, she may want to read the chapters which specifically pertain to her situation and skip certain other chapters.

It became rather clear during the process of writing Part Two that those chapters which deal with the stages of young adulthood, particularly those chapters concerned with students of high school or college age, are equally applicable to both sexes even at the present time. The same is true to some extent for the chapter dealing with working women and men and that dealing with preretirees and retirees.

Part Three serves as a practical resource, showing how to find a suitable volunteer job and including a detailed classification of different types of volunteer work. Also included in Part Three are descriptions of possible and sometimes out-of-the-ordinary volunteer projects which are particularly suitable for persons who like to work on their own, as well as a thorough explanation of various "hotlines" and self-help projects.

In the Appendixes one will find: descriptions of various counseling and testing services and referrals to specific volunteer counseling and placement offices; a sample worksheet (questionnaire), which helps in defining personal goals; instructions on preparing résumés; guidelines both for volunteers and for those who employ volunteer help, including a sample contract; and, last but not least, a comprehensive, nationwide list of volunteer groups (ranging sociopolitically from conservative to radical), as well as a list giving a resource network of national associations of professional women.

Cambridge, Massachusetts   H.L.
February 1974

Acknowledgments

Special thanks go to Marion Chase, my partner and codirector at the Civic Center and Clearing House, Inc., who made it possible for me to take a year's sabbatical; to Mary I. Bunting, former president of Radcliffe College, who was enthusiastic about this book and who wrote the Introduction for it; to Hans Hofmann for letting me defend my thesis before him; to Geno Ballotti of *Daedalus* who encouraged me to write, cheered me on, and set realistic deadlines for me; to Caroline Banks and Jeffrey Herman, whose moral support and editorial help were invaluable; to Sandra Kahn for conducting some of the interviews on which the profiles are based; to Helen Garvey for her patient and expert typing help; to Rachel Cox for producing the one guaranteed, delicious dinner a week for our family; and to the Radcliffe Institute where women receive strong support to carry out their individual projects and each is given a quiet place to work, "A Room of One's Own." Mary Albro, now of Smith College, advised me in the revision of the Worksheet. Thanks are equally due to friends and colleagues, too numerous to mention, who took time off from their work to offer criticism, make suggestions, and refer me to new sources. A vote of thanks goes to all those who have allowed me to quote what at my request they have recorded in their own words. I want to express special appreciation to my editors at Beacon

Press, Lee, Lois, and Ray, and to Dick of the art department, whose enthusiasm, firm support, and friendly advice have made publishing this book a most pleasurable experience. And finally this series of thanks would not be complete without mentioning my children: Helen, who found her life's work through volunteer service in the Peace Corps; Harris, who has a way of bridging the generation gap and taught me to communicate more easily with his peers; and Tom, who, notwithstanding his mother's writing pains in his last year at home, has genuine understanding and respect for the equality of women's and men's work.

I am immensely grateful to my close friend, Inge Pavlowsky, who came from France to illustrate this book with her pen-and-ink drawings. Our friendship dates back to 1937, when we met at school in England. We have collaborated since that time on a small volume, *Since Then*, a collection of letters edited by my husband and me. Madame Pavlowsky graduated from the Royal College of Art in London and taught arts and crafts at Anna Freud's wartime nursery in England. She now lives near Paris with her husband and four daughters. Throughout her summer visit to Boston she observed and sketched. As a European, she was struck and inspired by the strong tradition here of volunteer participation at all levels. With perception, warmth, and wit, she recorded some of her impressions of American women at work.

Introduction

BY MARY I. BUNTING

Max Otto of the University of Wisconsin once spoke of the vitality and the value of ideas "which grow out of the life they are to serve." He said, "Watch a skilled workman who knows what he's about, or look in on anyone who is concerned to do well his part in the world's work, and you find ideas in operation which are native to the activities they direct. They are overtones of general experience, standards of workmanship derived from long experimental practice, ways of bringing thought to the assistance of muscle in rising to the challenge of a job. This working principle of developing ideas out of the tasks that need doing, and testing them by their effectiveness then and there, seems to me the most promising strategy for life at large."

This is the basic strategy that Herta Loeser has used in writing *Women, Work, and Volunteering*. Her ideas about voluntarism, about women's lives, and about the relationships between them were developed directly from her own life experiences, her teaching, and her work as codirector of the Civic Center and Clearing House, Inc. For seven years she "interviewed, counseled, and placed hundreds of people and kept records of their progress." She thought and acted, observed and reflected. Hers is the wisdom of the craftsman. Her ideas as well as her data will be of immediate assistance to countless other individuals in search of a new direction or a new meaning in life.

Herta Loeser is a social activist, not a social scientist. The reader must look elsewhere for a history of voluntarism. The book makes no pretense, even in the introductory chapter, of giving a historical perspective; but future historians will find in it invaluable insights as well as a wealth of information about many aspects of life in this country during the 1960s and 70s. By the same token, the book has little to offer the scientist searching for a wealth of data, detailed analytical treatments, or new conceptual propositions; but it does provide ideas and personal experiences with which future theorists must deal.

The intended audience is the woman who, for one or more reasons, is looking for a more satisfying way to use some of her time; but a far wider assortment of readers will find the book interesting and valuable. Professional women, husbands, and the young, among others, will gain a better realization of the potentialities of volunteering for the individuals involved and for society. The inclusion of a few more examples of women whose early motivation was more positive and whose career development led to positions of notably significant influence and/or national leadership might have strengthened this interpretive function. I think of my own mother who began as a very part-time volunteer at the Brooklyn YWCA, became its president, then president of the National Board during the early 40s when the YWCA took a leading role in racial integration. She also served on the Board of Higher Education of New York City from 1938 to 1968 and was chairman of its "Committee to Look to the Future," which proposed major reorganizations. Volunteering undoubtedly gave my mother fully as much leverage and personal satisfaction over a longer period of years as any paid position or political career could have provided, and it did so on her terms, terms that permitted her to schedule her time away from home flexibly, according to her needs and those of her family.

Employers who have occasion to evaluate the potentialities of applicants who present nontraditional sequences of educational, job, and volunteer experiences will find it worthwhile to study *Women, Work, and Volunteering* with an eye to the opportunities for decision making, group leadership, broad contacts, stick-to-itiveness, etc., that volunteering can provide. Very frequently in academia I hear deans and college presidents remark that some older woman may be just a fresh Ph.D. but demonstrates, on such and such a committee, the management judgments and political insights one expects from an experienced professor. They had not appreciated what the woman had learned from her volunteer activities in the community. I know that my own experiences in helping to organize a regional school district were of inestimable value when I unexpectedly entered college administration as dean of Douglass College, and that close association with young adolescents in the home was wonderfully good preparation for coping with student unrest at Radcliffe in the late 60s. There is growing evidence that it may be an asset to include on one's staff people who have gained their experience in a variety of ways and on different timetables.

Perhaps an even more important function of Herta Loeser's book will be to ease the nagging doubts and crippling internal conflicts of women who do (but do not believe they should) find satisfaction in their volunteer activities. The positive case that she makes in such a balanced way, with so many authentic examples, legitimizes their choices. It can liberate such women and their families and perhaps some of their critics from the currently modish stereotypic thinking that tends to scorn unpaid work in the home, the community, or, sometimes with reason, in any established service organization.

As is all too often the case, the author's sense of balance and basic integrity will undoubtedly win her more enemies than friends. She takes her stand both for women's liberation and for voluntarism without dodging the hard issues, fudging the answers, or belittling those who hold other views. Although obviously not entirely satisfied that she has resolved the question, her willingness to tackle it, not just once but in several contexts, makes for some of the liveliest passages in the volume.

Even the early proponents of women's liberation have come to see that improving women's lot depends on fundamental changes in lifestyles, in concepts of family, and in a wide spectrum of relationships between members of both sexes. Herta Loeser never doubted this and never loses sight of the fact that models proposed for and adopted by women will not only affect men's lives but can eventually prove attractive and useful to them.

Many forces are at work in our society to make the central topic of this book of increasing importance. Especially in this country we have relied on rapid growth in population, education, and use of resources to open opportunities for interesting employment and fulfill the promise of democracy as we interpreted it. Such growth could not continue indefinitely, as the energy crisis has begun to convince us. What are the possibilities for creativity, for initiative, for working toward more satisfying lives of improved quality in a world in which key physical resources are in limited supply? I suspect that for many individuals and perhaps for society as a whole the answers will come fully as much from the field of volunteering as from the field of paid employment. The creative aspects of the lives of many men as well as many women will depend on the time and effort they can give and the recognition they can gain from unpaid artistic, scholarly, scientific, and social endeavors. Many business and professional leaders know this to be true and plan their time to include volunteer activities, but these are apt to be chosen opportunistically, without very careful analyses of costs or benefits. Herta Loeser's book may be only a beginning, but it is dealing with a far more important problem than its modest approach suggests.

Women, Work, and Volunteering is a how-to-do-it book with a difference. There is a sureness of touch that comes from long experience in counseling women, a balance that testifies to a mind that is tough as well as open, curious as well as concerned. There is the vitality as well as the wisdom of a craftsman dealing with working principles indigenous to the subject. There is a glimpse of a new social order that could be the wave of the future.

PART ONE

The Case for Volunteering

The motto of life is "give and take."
Everyone must be both a giver and a receiver.
He who is not both is a barren tree.

—Martin Buber in *Tales of the Hasidim*

1

Today's Volunteer Scene: A Preview

Volunteering, the free giving of one's time and talents for work deemed socially or politically beneficial, has become a controversial subject! A proponent of volunteering can no longer write about how, where, and when to volunteer, without first coming to grips with whether women should be urged to volunteer at all. And a writer like me, who believes that the feminist movement is necessary and must succeed, has the added burden of justifying her advocacy of volunteering in the face of the distrust of it felt by many in the feminist movement.

One of the dangers of our age, I think, is that our expertise at finding what's wrong with our institutions runs too far ahead of our ability to substitute better institutions. Even worse, we seem excessively ready to tear down entire structures because of their imperfections, without first asking ourselves whether the gap that will be created leaves us in better or worse shape. This *could* happen to volunteering. It would be enormously sad if it did, for I have no doubt that it would leave our society more barren and would leave many women *and* men unnecessarily deprived of stimulation, satisfaction, happiness, indeed, their sanity.

One way to guard against such mistakes, particularly when dealing with so pragmatic and practical a subject as volunteering, is to avoid too much theory and stay close to reality, to today's facts. So let me start, by way of a sampling from real life, to explain what it is that I call "volunteering."

My own volunteer job gives me familiarity with the whole spectrum of Boston's volunteer scene. For the past eight years I have helped first to rejuvenate and then to run a volunteer clearinghouse in Boston, a place where people of all ages and from many walks of life come for guidance, counseling, and placement in volunteer jobs. Our task is to match the personal talents and needs of individuals to the truly enormous requirements of our society for talent freely given.

My examples drawn from experience are valid beyond Boston, for I know that many of the same opportunities — though not always similar guidance, counseling, and placement services — exist in most other metropolitan and even some rural areas. Spurred by the example of Boston-area women, the Wilmington housewife, the Chicago nurse, the Seattle secretary will all gain motivation for volunteer work and discover possibilities they didn't know existed.

Last June a young reporter preparing to write an article on volunteer opportunities around town was impressed to find that she could take her pick of volunteer work from fifteen agencies virtually on her doorstep. A children's art center needed a ceramics teacher, the camping association was looking for extra counselors and for office help to cope with a flood of applications. The community schools — using the facilities of public school buildings during afternoons, evenings, and weekends — had openings for volunteer teachers of guitar, piano, creative writing, public speaking, pottery, sewing, yoga, and photography. The Cambridge Civic Association, a nonpartisan local political group that supports candidates for city offices, needed a writer for its newsletter. Education Warehouse, which prepares adults for high school equivalency diplomas and teaches English as a second language, could put to work all the volunteer tutors they could enlist. The Red Cross was looking for volunteers for their blood-donor room. A neighborhood settlement house needed a group worker. A drug rehabilitation program about to start a new training course was looking for more volunteer counselors. Both a physical therapist and a medical librarian were wanted for volunteer slots at one of the local hospitals. A legal aid office had several openings for pre-law students, and men and women were needed to stand by and help recently released prisoners.

But that's only the beginning. Any good directory of volunteer jobs in and around a city would include between 200 and 300 organizations and self-help groups. The richness of the volunteer opportunities which they offer is overwhelming.

For one interested in and able to handle the special challenges of inner-city programs, there are librarians' jobs in mostly black public schools where no libraries previously existed and openings for reading and arithmetic tutors and for teachers of English as a second language. There is a need for community health aides, dietitians, comparative shoppers, low-cost housing rehabilitation crews, and social work case-aides. Interpreters for court or clinic work, especially for the Spanish-speaking, are in great demand and short supply. Volunteers are constantly needed for drug, pregnancy, and VD counseling. And then there are any number of volunteer tasks related to environmental problems: one can work at controlling smokestack or airplane emissions, can organize a cleanup and continued upkeep of a neighborhood or playground, research the distribution of shade trees in different sections of a city as a basis for future plantings, study river pollution, work on dump control and relocation, or recycle paper, glass, and cans. One may join any number of legislative groups in their lobbying efforts. The Audubon Society, the Sierra Club, the League Against Sonic Booms, or one of the groups promoting bicycle riding, even prior to the gasoline shortage, all rely heavily on volunteer workers.

As for hospitals, there are over fifty in the Boston area, and all of them recruit volunteers. Some offer imaginative and creative placements within the hospital or in the adjacent community served by the hospital. Two hospitals, for example, have joined forces to provide English instruction for their foreign-born maintenance and kitchen crews. Volunteers go to the kitchens and do the teaching on location. Mental health agencies, correctional reform programs, organizations for the prevention of blindness and for the blind, the deaf, and the handicapped in general, all are searching for volunteers to work with people on a person-to-person basis.

There are art-related jobs in museums, art centers, and craft workshops; jobs with dance, music, opera, and theater groups; and jobs in connection with educational radio and television. If a volunteer possesses special knowledge or training, a resourceful counselor can find the right outlet to put such talent to work. Language proficiency? A number of international agencies rely almost completely on volunteers. Architectural history? A citywide survey of certain types of wrought-iron work, of various kinds of chimneys, mansards, and gables, and a research paper on the findings, perhaps with photographs, or even a documentary film, may be just what the local historical society would like to commission in support of a preservation bill.

It is often possible to combine training in one field with interest in another. A bookkeeper or secretary before marriage, now greatly intrigued with arts and crafts but with few skills in these fields, might enjoy being the volunteer office-business manager of an arts and crafts center, a local art association, or a children's museum.

Many such opportunities are discussed more specifically in Part Two. For the moment, these samples are enough to give the flavor of what volunteering can be and to show that volunteering has gone far beyond the more traditional activities, such as stuffing, stamping, and mailing envelopes; ringing doorbells during political campaigns; running bazaars and fairs for charities and schools; PTA chores; or taking the

cashier's place in a hospital coffee or gift shop. I do not belittle
this core of older, established volunteer activities; it gets work
done that needs to be done and gives satisfaction to many who
do it. Yet frequently it also gives rise to the sense of frustration
which surfaces in the comment I hear over and over again: "I

have done all the volunteer work I ever want to do. Now I want to do some *real* work."

Volunteer counselors like me have learned to be careful about judgments concerning specific organizations and their long-held reputations. Certain garden clubs no longer are what they used to be. Some are working to develop hardier varieties of decorative cabbage plants which, as potted plants in city window boxes and flowerbeds, can survive city exhaust fumes and cheer up thousands of passers-by who live or work in the city. The vest-pocket parks, the "plant mobiles" crisscrossing town in the summer bringing living things to city youngsters and teaching them how to grow and care for them are modernized versions of the good old garden club syndrome. And if this doesn't resemble your local garden club, then how about volunteering to help bring its activities up to date?

The Association of Junior Leagues, an international organization of more than 100,000, is, even now, too often viewed as a group of privileged women trying "to do good." Yet today Junior League members serve as trained and supervised volunteers who will take on difficult projects and will pitch in and stick with even the most demanding tasks. We must be very careful, then, to insure that our image of such organizations is not stereotyped but truly accurate.

2

The Changing Use of Time

Our volunteer scene could not have been described as I have just done, twenty or even ten years ago, let alone fifty or a hundred years ago. The changes taking place in volunteering, as in everything else, are breathtaking. And they are, of course, closely related to other changes in the world around us.

For those of us raised on Aldous Huxley, and more recently exposed to *Future Shock* by Toffler, it is a truism that the rate of change in our society is continuously accelerating. This rapidity of change is at the root of many of our most serious problems as a society.

In times like these, history may be an unreliable guide to the future. Volunteering has been an important factor throughout the social history of America. In the past, it has adapted with relative success to changing conditions. Yet, if this is one of the few books on volunteering which does not quote de Tocqueville's view of the importance of volunteer activities in American society, the omission is intentional. We can no longer assume that the proven historical ability of a tradition like volunteering to adapt to changing conditions establishes volunteering as a viable social force for the future. My conviction that it will be, therefore, requires more explanation.

Our use of *time* is undergoing a fundamental change, not just a change in degree but a profound change in kind. What the volunteer gives is also *time*. This interrelationship is important.

In seconds or less the computer does tasks that used to take hours, perhaps days — or were not practical at all because of the time involved. We fly to London in seven hours. Only thirty years ago most travelers had to go by ship and took twenty-four times as long. Rocket-propelled Americans and Russians presently fly through space at twenty to thirty times the speed of the London jet — spanning the Boston-London distance in about fifteen minutes. Computer- and tape-controlled typing machines can produce finished material, error free, in less time than it took the secretary to take the material down in shorthand. The use of time in a highly computerized modern factory differs as much from Henry Ford's expectations as his assembly lines differed from pre-industrial production schedules.

The effect on human work patterns of all these ways to do more in less time is only just beginning to be felt. The details are still experimental, but the direction is clear. Fewer people will be working fewer hours to produce a given amount of goods or services.

The 40-hour week is certainly on the way out. Indeed, on a closer look it is obvious that the 40-hour week standard has been a myth in many a business for years. The typical 9-5 office day with an hour for lunch and two fifteen-minute coffee breaks, five days a week, adds up to only 32½ hours of work per week. Holidays and vacations reduce the average even further. The large unionized employers are moving away from the 40-hour week, some toward fewer hours in a standard day, some toward a four and a half- or four-day week. A shorter work week at full pay levels will become reality for millions of people in the near future.

Retirement, too, is coming earlier to more and more people.

Yet men and women live longer. Earlier retirement is here to stay. The unions are pushing for it, and management sees its advantages. Thirty percent of manufacturing firms now offer liberalized benefits to those who retire before 65, nearly double the percentage of a decade ago. The quicker turnover of the human work force is due, in part, to the pressure from below to make room for younger and usually lower-paid workers.

So far I have emphasized the influence of technology on the changing workweek and working lifetime. But fundamental changes in human expectations will have at least as great an effect on our changing work patterns. Both factors push us in the same direction.

There is increased dissatisfaction with the dullness and routine of many jobs. Relative affluence carries with it the luxury of being able to question the quality and the content of one's job. Many believe that the sky-high absenteeism, staggering personnel turnover rates, and the low effective working hours which plague industry are directly related to boredom on the job.

Very few people can enjoy on their jobs the thrill of accomplishing a difficult task, of doing something they never dreamed they could do. Rising to a challenge is apt to bring out the very best in people, and yet few jobs ever provide that opportunity.

Insofar as I can gather from conflicting analyses, increased automation will not solve this problem. It will eliminate some drudge jobs, but not all; and it may create new ones. All indications are that, for most people, the remedy will have to be new opportunities to engage in interesting tasks outside of their work routine. The trend is here now; there will be more training and study on the boss's time, more sabbaticals, an increase in "released time," all intended to help nurture the spirit.

None are more outspoken in their hesitation to devote a

lifetime to corporate routine than the young. A much greater proportion than ever before are as concerned with the purpose, content, and challenge of a job as with its financial rewards. If they cannot find a job which is satisfactory by those standards, some choose to drive a taxi, wait on tables, clean houses, or work as orderlies, guards, or other service-oriented jobs for part of their time, in order to be able to do what they consider more challenging or socially useful work the rest of the week. Vocations for Social Change publishes the *People's Yellow Pages* to assist in that sort of approach to a new lifestyle. The 1973 edition focuses on the "Exploration of the Meanings of Work."* Many young people do not foresee sticking with any one occupation or career for the rest of their lives.

Following the lead of the younger generation, a growing number of their elders are taking a second look at the value of their life's work. Some decide to quit the rat race and make a sharp change in their own lifestyles. Switches to second careers which seemed improbable and impractical only a short while ago are no longer isolated instances.

Employers and unions must and will become increasingly flexible to accommodate these new work patterns. And the greatest pressures for change in this area will come from women. So far, as Matina Horner, president of Radcliffe College, recently noted, "although the social structure decries the terrible loss of female potential in both economic and personal terms, it provides few, if any positive incentives or sanctions for career-oriented women."** Not only will increasing opportunities have to be provided for women at the usual

---

*People's Yellow Pages, 1973 edition, Vocations for Social Change. V.S.C. is a program of the New England Regional Office of the American Friends Service Committee.

**Matina S. Horner, "Femininity and Successful Achievement: a Basic Inconsistency," *Feminine Personality and Conflict* (Belmont, California: Brooks/Cole Publishing Company, 1970), p.46.

entry points to careers, but work patterns must be established that will routinely permit permanent part-time work, as well as reentry into former careers at later life stages and entry into new "second careers."

Team management by two people jointly holding one executive or administrative job promises exciting possibilities for employees and employers alike. My agency is run by two women acting as codirectors, making it possible for each to work part-time. Two of us share the full executive responsibility and provide full-time supervisory staffing. We are satisfied that our two halves add up to more than just One, in terms of delivery of service and output. This pattern of executive teamwork is readily transferrable to business, as several enterprising and flexible employers are finding out for themselves. It has a real future!

The new living patterns which are evolving among young families decisively influence all of the trends I have described. Many families are experimenting with quite a different work distribution between husbands and wives than has been customary. Both men and women do their share of housekeeping and child raising, giving women a greater chance to succeed at work outside the home. Massachusetts Institute of Technology has recently hired a husband-and-wife team as codirectors of its Office of Personnel Development. Each will work part time.

The increasing mobility of our work force also effects changes in work patterns. Modern communications have made this an ever smaller country in people's minds, and moving from one end to the other is an accepted practice for many families. There is an obvious price paid for this in the cutting of emotional ties, the hesitancy to form attachments for fear of having to break them again, and the resultant feeling of rootlessness.

Many of the changes in work patterns we have considered exact a price and create new problems — but they also open vast new opportunities. Let us look at this balance between problems and opportunities.

According to a study of national life made in 1972 by Japan's Economic Planning Agency, the average Japanese male works from young manhood to old age, uses his spare time to improve work skills, and rarely takes either vacation or sick leave. Only 20 percent of Japanese workers, it is said, actually take the paid vacation to which they are entitled. Their reason: they are accustomed to working all the time and do not enjoy or know what to do with leisure.

Though these extreme attitudes are not typical for Americans, most of us have within us many of the same fears that motivate the Japanese. As Robert S. Weiss says in *Work and Automation: Problems and Prospects,* "Although it is generally assumed that the Germans and the Swiss work harder than Americans, it is doubtful that there are any other people on earth to whom work is as important to [one's] self." The prospect of enforced idleness, or put more positively, of increased leisure time, is very frightening to many people. In this respect the futurologists' predictions of only a couple of decades ago are catching up with us fast. Moonlighting jobs are harder and harder to come by, as more people want to use their spare time for a second and even a third job. Conversely, marriages of 20, 25, and 30 years' duration often feel the strain of too much togetherness.

These fears and problems are not new. We have long been aware of them in connection with 65- to 70-year-old retirees. What is new is that these problems will hit more and more people of all ages. When we add together the shortened work week, earlier retirement, longer life expectancies, women's unwillingness to be mere housekeepers, youngsters with terms-off (even years-off) from studies, the sum of newly available hours not needed for the main job is staggering. And staggering, too, are the opportunities that beckon.

We are just beginning to grasp these possibilities —

including the immensity of the risk that this vast new reservoir should remain almost untapped. There is real danger that people will fritter away the new free time on the mechanics of living, on busywork (Parkinson's Law in reverse?), on activities that waste time without increasing the happiness of either the individual or the group in society.

As one of my students, a young mother, puts it, "At present my children take up almost all of my time. But soon the morning will be mine, and I know that if I don't find some challenging occupation, that time will be absorbed by housework that will automatically expand to fill it."

The opportunity then, is for people to learn to guard and treasure this new-found time, and to use it for the pursuit of more personal fulfillment: education, hobbies, art, and, of course, sports. But it is hoped that people will find also a whole new world of interests involving service to other humans. And that gets us to volunteer work.

3

If Volunteering Didn't Survive, It Would Have to Be Re-invented

Each of our days still contains twenty-four hours, of which at least sixteen are waking hours. Less than a century ago the average working person spent three quarters of that waking time in making a living, on at least six days of each week. More recently, only half of those waking hours were taken up by the job, and on only five days of the week. Soon the average of daily work hours may approach only five to six waking hours, and the job will take up only four days a week.

The converse is important for our purposes: two to three days out of every seven-day week will be wholly free of job burdens, as will be well over half of the waking hours of every workday. Add to this the other trends mentioned before—more vacation, earlier retirement, less time needed to accomplish the necessaries of life, etc.—and the capital question all this poses is obvious: What happens to all this "free" time?

Derek Bok, president of Harvard University, expressed his hope in his welcoming address to the incoming freshmen, in September 1972, that they would keep these objectives in mind: (1) the pursuit of a career or vocation that will truly exercise their talents; (2) sufficient leisure time for aesthetic, athletic, and intellectual pursuits; and (3) a sensitivity to the problems of others and a willingness to spend substantial time and energy in the service of their fellow human beings. In short, a full life should encompass these three segments: work, play, and service to others.

As we have seen, the work segment of one's time is contracting, and the available leisure time is growing correspondingly. Thus we must assume that more and more time will become available for play and for service to others.

The idea of having less work and more free time sounds thrilling at first. Yet on closer examination it provides one more factor of uncertainty and yet another break with tradition.

I know of two companies which have recently explored plans for a shorter workweek. The employees of one company, when given a choice, turned down the shorter workweek. The other firm, an insurance company, is now cautiously extending its original experiment and is giving more employees the option of a shorter workweek.

Why don't all employees jump at the chance of less work with no reduction in pay? The answers are complex, and probably include the deep-seated conviction that in the long run less work must mean less pay, a conviction reflected in union policies to date. But no one doubts that there is also a strong intuitive fear of too little work and too much playtime. The good old work ethic is still deeply embedded.

I cannot agree that work, any kind of work, is good per se, notwithstanding the recent flurry of reaffirmations of that old belief by those highest in our government. Clearly, I see no great intrinsic merit in monotonous work resulting in production of nonessential goods and services.

But the reverse is also undesirable: idleness and play alone do not satisfy the human soul. We all sense that more than play is needed to keep us satisfied. Otherwise we feel blunted and bloated, as after a large meal. We tend to thrive on challenge, to appreciate variety, and to need contrasts.

"All work and no play makes Jack a dull boy . . ." may have to be reversed to "all play and no work makes Jack . . . ." We feel best when we can fulfill demands made on us. We enjoy leisure and playtime much better and use it more creatively after having labored hard.

Thus our own inner needs push us toward the third component: service to others.

We have focused on the needs of individuals to find ways to fill part of their leisure from the job with useful work. At the same time, we know that the needs of our society are staggering. Poverty is rampant in the midst of plenty. Facilities serving the handicapped and the sick desperately need help, as do our penal institutions. More and more people are making new demands on cultural centers of all kinds, but these institutions lack adequate funds to provide extended and urgently needed services. We have to worry about the air we breathe, the water we drink or swim in, the pesticides which show up in our livestock and our food, the noise which assails our ears and bombards our sensitivities. Wildlife is endangered everywhere in the world and needs rescuing. The energy crisis proves without doubt that we must work out saner modes of mass transportation within the city and between cities. We are warned that we shall soon wallow in our own garbage, yet we must not increase air pollution by incinerating refuse.

The list of societal needs which committed human beings can help alleviate is immense. And the personal need of men and women to find satisfying secondary work and interests is also growing at a greatly accelerated rate. For once, the important trends that concern us are complementary, not divergent.

At this point, the volunteer's hand appears to fit the glove of our needs almost too perfectly. It is tempting to overstate the case for volunteering. Some cautionary comments are in order.

Volunteering is an obvious, necessary, and, I believe constructive response to the individual and societal needs of today and the forseeable future. But it is by no means the only answer to the problems on which this book has touched, nor even necessarily the most important response. Much needs to be done to make jobs themselves more interesting and satisfying. We need to shift some of our enthusiasm from spectator to participatory sports. Free time should be filled in part with interest in hobbies, arts, crafts, music. Reading may in turn stimulate greater concern with governmental short-comings, the need for better services. The list is endless.

The proliferation of adult and continuing education courses, the projected open universities (already in existence in England, and now in Massachusetts), greatly facilitated travel opportunities, all are indicative of the pressures for new outlets for surplus time and energy.

If I harp on volunteering here, it is because that is what this book is about, not because I am blind to, or want to downgrade, other problems and needed responses. And as we shall see in the next chapter, the very same pressures which have been mentioned are also effecting changes in volunteering itself, by bringing in new types of volunteers and opening up new opportunities for them.

4

The Changing State of Volunteering

We have seen that we live at a time when there are both a vast public need for volunteers and an increasing personal need to be a volunteer. Supply and demand appear to move in unison. Yet keeping them roughly in step will require imagination, innovation, and flexibility on both sides of the equation.

There is already much innovation. Entirely new categories of volunteers are being created, and new sources of volunteers are being tapped.

Some forward-looking companies now have programs for the release of a small number of their employees during the day to do volunteer work in the community on company time. Sometimes these "paid volunteers" are chosen because they already volunteer on their own time after hours, and the company is willing to match those hours — just as many companies match their employees' charitable donations. A very few business firms go further, offering paid leaves of absence for six months or longer so that employees may follow through on a community project of their choice. It is my understanding that the Xerox Corporation, for example, guarantees employees on such sabbaticals a return to the job held previously without loss of seniority.

What the Germans call "Gleitzeit" (gliding time or Flex-time) is now beginning to move from Europe to this country. Recent statistics show that "Flex-time," first introduced in Germany in 1967, is being adopted by more American companies all the time and that some 85,000 Americans (in 45 companies) are involved in the experiment. Though it involves no released time, it allows employees flexibility in scheduling their workday. Typically, such employees are free to begin their workday anytime between 8 a.m. and 10 a.m., and to regulate their lunch periods and quitting time correspondingly, just so long as the total number of hours worked equals the established norm of seven hours per day, or 35 hours in five days. Such flexibility greatly facilitates volunteer commitments by employees. For example, by beginning early on two days a week, the employee can make a commitment to a volunteer job at 4:30 p.m. on each of those days, and yet can sleep later on other mornings if he or she chooses.

Persons who take advantage of any of these new business programs often bring very special skills to their volunteer work — and are likely to be achievement-oriented in the limited time at their disposal — perhaps unique in their lifetime if it is a sabbatical or the like. More importantly, this sort of program tends to infuse men into volunteer work that produces service or social change (or sometimes both).

More and more men of all ages are volunteering in direct service jobs, where previously they have tended to serve mostly on boards of directors and in political capacities. Except for a few programs like the Big Brothers and the Boy Scouts, which have always attracted male volunteers, men have only recently become involved in such activities as recording books for the blind, tutoring emotionally disturbed children, working in day-care centers, and assisting as school volunteers in elementary or high schools.

This trend is important. It is of obvious benefit to the clients served, be they boys or girls, men or women, lending needed balance to the services rendered. But it is also of vital importance to the future of volunteering as an institution, as I explain in the next chapter, wherein I face the often alleged conflict between volunteering and the women's movement. The more men join the mainstream of volunteering, the greater will be the acceptability of volunteering in our modern society. The Peace Corps and VISTA have attracted thousands of young men and are now open to older men volunteers with particular skills. One-, two-, and three-year terms of voluntary service are not unusual. VITA (Volunteers for International Technical Assistance) draws on the talents of professional men for consulting work here and abroad. Many of the alumni of these volunteer programs can be counted on to continue the habit.

There is yet another new way in which men now become involved in service to individuals: men in business accept responsibility for volunteer student interns. This gives the students their first opportunity to take a realistic look at the workaday world. The independent study project, flexible campus plan, and many of the other programs described in Part Two, Chapter 7, on the "term off"or the "year off," could not begin to function without the businessmen's willingness to plan, make room, and take time out for these student interns, and to guide and supervise them.

As for the young themselves, more and more they are asking to be allowed to play their part in the world outside the classroom. Volunteering, in one way or another, has become a way of life with many of them. "School-without-walls" programs are perhaps at their peak of popularity right now. Poor placements and spotty followup will hasten the demise of some of these programs; but when the fad element subsides, as it will, the many positive aspects of the best of these programs can be emphasized and consolidated. The young have been urging us by radical and not so radical means to make them an integral and important part of the community.

They have also been urging us to take another look at "how we have always done things," and these educational experiments represent a partial response to that pressure. Even the Scouting movement is adjusting its image and through its "Explorers" program now draws resources from the entire community. The "High School Student" and "The Undergraduate" sections in this book deal in more detail with the volunteer involvement of young adults.

Volunteering is habit forming. What you learn when young is likely to stay with you for life. This can and should include the habit of serving others, of volunteering. The earlier boys and girls get started on voluntary service, the more likely they are to make it an integral part of their whole lives.

Experience indicates that men and women who have not had exposure to volunteer work are far less likely than those who have had such experience to be successful when, as senior citizens, they wish to take up volunteering. *"Frueh uebt sich was ein Meister werden will"* ("Early practice makes the master"). Retirees who can draw on the experience of a lifetime of community involvement will naturally continue to be active, concerned, and unlikely to be bored in later life. Without such preconditioning, many unavoidably fall instead into the role of uninvolved observers of the scene, or become disenchanted and bitter members of society. Why should a man or a woman wait for retirement before coming forward to volunteer? The habit should be established early. That is the best possible preparation for successful participation in the many programs such as Foster Grandparents, RSVP, VITA, SCORE, and so forth, which attempt to use the skills and experience of the elderly for the well-being of society and, simultaneously, for their own well-being.

Back to women volunteers: The nonworking woman, the housewife with time on her hands, usually comes to mind first. Yet there are thousands of working women who volunteer in the evenings and on weekends. Often their requests for volunteer jobs are hard to fill, simply because we are not yet flexible enough in our institutions to accommodate them, though we should and must. Airline stewardesses have free days between flights, and many are anxious to offer their services in the community. Here, too, extra imagination and flexibility are needed to accommodate their schedules, but it can be done.

Another relatively new source of competent volunteers comes from the families mentioned before who are mobile and have just recently moved into the community — whether for two years, five years, or for good, they themselves may not know. These men and women have had to cut emotional ties when they left their former location; they crave new relationships but are also afraid of them because they are unsure whether the new human commitments will be allowed to last. Volunteering offers these men and women new contacts with other people and insights into the needs of their new community, together with the possibility of making a commitment to do something about these needs. And since it all starts out on a quasi-professional, structured basis, the potential human ties can be cautiously tested. It is comparatively easy to retract into the safety of one's own shell, and increasingly greater human involvement can readily be paced at a rate that is comfortable. These newcomer families are good sources of capable volunteers, and once again they tend to provide more and more male volunteers for service jobs.

New types of volunteers often require a new adaptability on the part of the employing agencies. I have already referred to the need for nighttime and weekend volunteer openings for full-time workers, and for even more flexible scheduling to accommodate such groups as flight personnel. But more basically, *we must facilitate the transition from volunteer work to paid work and back again.* At different stages in their lives, people will want, and should be able, to gravitate between different kinds of work, paid and unpaid, as their circumstances require. What is needed are a sliding scale, a graduation of work experiences, an openness, which will allow easy shifts from one mode of work to the other.

Voluntary work can be structured so as to take up the slack between temporary jobs — at the very time when more people elect to take temporary jobs.

Barbara is a case in point. She takes a temporary job only when she needs the income to help pay for her son's college expenses, and between jobs she is a freelance volunteer taking her choice of assignments. During the last year she completed a research study for a large general hospital, pinch-hit for the vacationing director of the Volunteer Action Center, and is now conducting training sessions for volunteer staff members. As this illustration shows, a person can alternate between paid and unpaid work during the course of a single year. Some hold paid and unpaid jobs simultaneously; others may prefer to alternate between them.

Perhaps the greatest flexibility is needed to accommodate the largest and most important untapped volunteer source of all, the potential volunteers from the inner city neighborhoods, the less affluent members of society. Our very recent history tells us that some of the most needed skills and talents lie dormant among those who are often thought of only as recipients of volunteer efforts. This group has as much to give as to gain by change-oriented volunteering. Grassroots workers, members of tenant councils and other political-action groups, community health workers, neighborhood school and library aides are all the more effective because of the intimate knowledge they have of their community. A lot of thought is currently being given to the possibility, the necessity, of offering financial subsidies to these volunteers, to whom carfare, child care, and lunch expenses would otherwise be prohibitive obstacles. I have little patience with the purists' objections to even minimal subsidies of that kind; they perceive the danger that such subsidies might undermine the "voluntary" aspect of citizen and community action. Competition between paraprofessional neighborhood workers and subsidized volunteer workers sometimes creates an additional complication. On the whole, however, I have found that these problems loom far larger in planning sessions than in practice in the field. Usually they can be worked out in a practical way. Paid staff, paraprofessionals, and volunteers all have their place; full mutual acceptance has not yet been achieved, and the labor unions (particularly hospital labor unions) view this three-pronged approach (paid staff, paraprofessionals, and volunteers) with apprehension.

There is no question that until recently volunteering has been almost exclusively confined to upper-middle- and upper-income-bracket classes. In my view, its inability to attract large numbers from the lower end of the socio-economic scale has been its greatest weakness. There are some exciting indications now that shorter work periods without loss of pay, and increased activism among all classes, will bring these long-missed men and women into community activities on a volunteer basis. I hope so. It would greatly enrich the volunteer scene, other volunteers, *and* their clients.

I have come to believe that volunteering in and of itself is, and should increasingly become, socially beneficial. As more and more men and women of all ages and from all walks of life work as volunteers, the volunteer scene itself can become an equalizing force, a platform for social intercourse, understanding, and change. We have a long way to go to accomplish that vision across the board, but we are making progress. The old social divisiveness between the "have" volunteer and the "have-not" client is becoming blurred. And I do not consider myself utopian when I foresee community decision making influenced greatly by community-based volunteers, from whose ranks can be drawn cadres of new locally based leaders.

Ultimately, and this *is* quite utopian, I would hope that as volunteering becomes a more widespread and accepted part of life for a greater spectrum of people, it might help shift our emphasis somewhat, away from monetary rewards and more toward other satisfactions gained from work that is worthwhile. As I look at the automated future forecast by so many, I think it is very possible that *being allowed* to work at something that makes sense, that is interesting and challenging and engages one's full potential — rather than merely gaining affluence and status — may indeed become the true privilege. If so, only volunteering on the broadest scale offers the hope that this privilege will be spread widely throughout our society, and will not result simply in a new hopeless class division between the new work elite and the drones doing nothing but the routine jobs.

5

Feminism and Volunteering

The women's movement represents, in my view, one of the few true revolutions — perhaps the only real one — in progress in present-day America. It must succeed. Yet the women's movement has become suspicious of volunteering, as yet another means by which our male-dominated society subverts women's liberation. Therefore I must justify my conviction that my advocacy of volunteering as an important means for many modern women to enrich their lives and those of others is entirely consistent with women's liberation.

There is, of course, no denying that the structure of many agencies which employ volunteers has historically reflected, and often still reflects, the male dominance we find throughout our society. Policy-making offices and board memberships are still held mostly by men, even in agencies where women do virtually all of the work. Thus I cannot disagree with the charge that much service-oriented volunteering has served so far to reaffirm stereotyped sex roles; that voluntary agencies have been a convenient safety valve for women's energies, giving an illusion of participation *but* no real power; that they have made it easier to keep some of the most effective women safely out of the labor market; and that they may even, by the dedicated, intelligent, and hard work of their women volunteers, have helped from time to time to ameliorate the most glaring faults in our society, thus preventing collapse but also deferring needed basic reforms.

I agree with those premises. But I disagree to the extent that anyone is led by these revelations to conclude that volunteering by women must be done away with, or must be restricted to change-oriented volunteering, in order to accomplish women's liberation. I disagree on grounds of logic, fundamental belief, and pragmatic need.

I said at the outset of this book that I worry about our inclination to do away with institutions that we find faulty, especially since we have found no adequate substitutes. This is a case in point. To argue that volunteering by women must go because it has so far served to reinforce male dominance of important portions of our society makes no better sense than arguing for the abolition of nurses, physiotherapists, and hospital social workers because American medicine has historically kept women confined to these supportive roles, thereby assuring male dominance of the top jobs and thus of medicine as a whole. Patently, as virtually all in the women's movement would agree, the remedy in medicine must be a loosening, an opening up, a new integration which brings many more women into the top medical jobs and also raises the status of the supportive jobs so as to make them attractive as careers for men *as well as* women. The remedy for volunteering, as we shall see, is not so different.

But I have an even more fundamental disagreement with those who jump too quickly from past abuses to the conclusion that volunteering is counterproductive for women now. The modern volunteering scene which I sketched in Chapter 1 was largely created by women. Whatever may be its faults to date insofar as woman's status is concerned, everything we know about the future indicates that here a lifestyle has been pioneered by women which will be right, indeed necessary, for women *and* men in the new society at our doorstep. I see the prospect that, under the stresses and frustrations of the women's revolution, we will kill what may potentially be one of woman's most perceptive and immediately useful contributions to future contentment for women *and* men.

In the man's world, achievement is usually rewarded with power and money, and those two give status which is often the ultimate reward. Women must gain equal access to that world, *and volunteering is no substitute*. With this I agree completely.

But there is much that is wrong with that man's world; we see its faults all around us. We cannot accept that world uncritically or become submerged in it without attempting to influence it.

Fortunately, the new technological and social pressures discussed in Chapter 2 combine at this point in history to allow men *and* women some time off from the pursuit of money and power, and to produce greater interest in seeking satisfaction by serving societal needs. Much of the criticism of volunteering ignores these trends. More and more time of both men and women will be devoted to activities other than those of money making. In such a world, volunteering must *expand*, not contract. At the same time, it must (and necessarily will) change with the rest of our society toward equality for women. As women achieve equality in the men's world outside volunteering, they will as a matter of course also enter the controlling jobs in volunteer organizations. Indeed, this is already happening, and even more quickly in many voluntary agencies than elsewhere in our society. And at the same time, as we have seen, many more men are entering the service end of volunteering. In short, there is now, and increasingly will be, the same loosening, the same opening up, and integration of men and women and of job status as in medicine and throughout other male-dominated job markets.

I do not counsel young women to be housewives and

volunteers, instead of following a career. I agree that it is important for women to be able to be economically independent. I do, however, believe that the following points are also valid: First, that gainfully employed women, like their male counterparts, can enrich their lives and those of others by also doing volunteer work. Second, that for many women who have never had, or have interrupted, a career, volunteering can offer a perfect transition back into full-time or part-time careers, and can be a fine way to experiment with just what mix is right. Third, that for many modern women, weaving back and forth between various roles, including those of volunteer and paid professional, can create a satisfying and interesting new lifestyle. And finally, that for many of today's women who, for better or for worse, have led the life principally of wife and mother, a heavy volunteer commitment can make all the difference in the world and can in fact help to make them freer and more liberated women.

This is a good point at which to insert a very special plea for tolerance on the part of the women's movement toward the particular needs of many middle-aged and older women. The women's movement has reached the consciousness of most women only in the last few years. Many who are thirty and up understand its aims intellectually and can support them — but that does not mean that all of these women are able to live to the hilt the new type of life suddenly open to and indeed demanded of them. Many of the factors that molded them were terribly wrong, but mold they did. And many of these women may find greater happiness and greater usefulness if they are allowed to live within what they perceive as their limitations, than if they are forced to strain beyond their personal capacity to compete as equals in the male world.

For these women — though certainly not *only* for these women — volunteering may offer an extraordinarily practical way out. If they are well counseled, they can use it to

determine how far they can press "equality," where their
limits are. They may thus use it as a bridge from mother and
housewife to full-time paid worker, or as a permanent
compromise between their aspirations and their personal
capacities, as they view them.

Thus I have no difficulty in concluding that the type of
volunteering which this book is about is wholly consistent
with women's liberation. But before I can leave this subject, I
must face another charge against volunteering — at least
service-oriented volunteering — often raised in the feminist
movement, though its scope is even greater than feminism. It
is said that volunteers tend not to help the underprivileged,
but to "put them in their place," and further that the more
effective the volunteers are, the better they patch up basic
faults in our system which should not be patched at all but
rather should be permanently replaced by fundamental
change. Change, it is argued, is thereby put off; therefore
women should no longer volunteer for service, but only for
political and social change.

There are still some voluntary agencies in which the Lady
Bountiful attitude lingers on, where comfortable ladies give
things or services and expect a gratefully pliable clientele in
return. My advice on that subject is simple: avoid such
agencies as you would the plague, unless you are the well-
organized, aggressive type who might enjoy the battle it
would take to change them around, to bring them in tune with
what we have learned since Florence Nightingale and even
Jane Addams. Good counselors know these agencies. The
volunteering I write about doesn't include these antedelu-
vians — though there are enough of them left to warrant a
caution here against blind commitments.

I do not agree that women should volunteer only for
political change or for change that directly benefits women.
The type of volunteering which we glimpsed in Chapter 2 is
forward looking and like all dynamic enterprises must be and

is change-oriented. Much excitement, much innovation, and much drive for change also are to be found in educational, medical, legal, scientific — in short, in service-oriented — volunteering.

Dealing with the second charge — that volunteering as an institution may prevent or delay needed social changes — is more complex. The charge has some merit, though the fault lies usually with those who misinterpret voluntarism, rather than with the voluntary agencies or the volunteers themselves.

I feel we are currently being treated to a gross misinterpretation of the concept of voluntarism by our own government. The present administration is giving publicity to voluntarism that distorts the purpose and meaning of volunteering. Voluntary action is being packaged and wholesaled for consumption like a commodity, while at the same time its real, often subtle, values to society are obliterated. It is time to question the motives behind a policy which leads the administration in Washington to use the public media for emotional appeals urging citizens to play their part in making the wheels of our society go around — appeals deliberately designed to arouse guilt feelings — when, at the same time, funding of the most urgent domestic social welfare programs is drastically cut back by that same administration. Voluntary action is never an alternative to government funding and responsibility; the trumpet call for volunteers must not drown out the clamor for massive financial support from the government for domestic needs, including health, education, and welfare, as well as for cultural institutions and programs. The federal, state, and local governments must not be allowed to abdicate their responsibility by attempts to shift the burden of performance to volunteers.

For the present, it is clear that many voluntary agencies in our society are forced to deal — inadequately, I think — with problems of basic poverty and of basic social and environmental needs. I have become convinced that only tax-supported programs can truly cope with these needs, if anything can. I favor efforts to change our system so that taxes *will* be used to meet such problems more fully. (In fact, the tough and long political battles needed to move in these directions themselves offer productive uses of volunteer power.) But, once again, I oppose carrying that argument to the ruthless, abstract conclusion often suggested — i.e., that since the patching job volunteers can do may delay the collapse that might force reform, we should cut off the volunteer effort. Such absolutes seldom do any good. I'll put it more strongly: the free choice to inflict avoidable suffering on human beings in order to hasten future change is seldom taken by those who are suffering. Therefore, the arrogance of such decision making deters me, particularly since the suffering is certain while the future benefits, which supposedly justify the means, are necessarily speculative — highly so in today's political climate.

In this area there must be moderation; there is much room for constructive compromise. The effective voluntary agency must continue to do its job as best it can, even while it also recognizes — particularly in its public relations and forward planning — that it must not cover up the shortcomings in its achievements, that it has a duty to highlight the areas where its resources are hopelessly inadequate to the task and where fundamental change is needed. Resourceful and intelligent leadership can maintain a sensitive balance between the immediate human needs requiring attention, which must come first, and the necessary long-range emphasis away from these hopeless problems which only government has the resources to solve.

The subject of this chapter is too diffuse to be summarized easily. Yet I would like to emphasize at least one consistent thread that runs through my attitude on these issues. Our world is predominantly a male world, in which we women demand equality. But it is also a world in which much is wrong. If all we do is join it, adopt its values uncritically, and perpetuate its wrongs, we shall have failed. Join it as equals we must and will, but I agree with Kay Boals that

>It is absolutely essential for the creation of a productive synthesis of masculine and feminine values in the culture that male attitudes and values change as well as those of women, for just as racism cannot be eliminated solely by changes in the attitudes of blacks, so sexism and the pervasive cultural denigration of the feminine cannot be transformed solely by changes in female attitudes and values.*

This means the infusion into the decision-making and style-setting layers of our society of humanizing female qualities of strength. I happen to think that the best of our volunteer efforts reflect a heavy dose of these qualities. We would render a massive disservice to society as a whole if we sacrificed these, our own creation, to short-range expediency. In the long run, as Kay Boals puts it

>Our efforts will be in vain unless men are willing to join in the struggle to create a society in which both males and females will be free to participate equally, and in which traits heretofore considered feminine are seen as essential to the full humanity of all of us and of society as a whole.**

We must not forget that it is up to us to lead in that direction.

*Kay Boals, "On Getting Feminine Qualities into the Power Structure," *University: A Princeton Quarterly*, no. 54 (Fall 1972), pp. 6-12.
**Ibid.*

6

The Idea of the Volunteer Professional

So far we have looked at the institution of volunteering generally — the reasons for it in the past, present, and near-future, and some objections to it. I have stood solidly in support of more voluntarism as a positive response to the needs and pressures of our time. From here on I shall particularize. In Part Two of the book, I will attempt to apply these general conclusions to the specific needs and abilities of people — women in particular, but not exclusively — in various life situations.

As I have repeatedly indicated, much of what I have to say applies only to the serious volunteer, the "volunteer professional," who considers her volunteer job as an important commitment in her life. The way she looks upon her work, and the way she is looked upon at her work, are crucial factors. They are factors which pervade virtually all the specific volunteer roles in the rest of this book.

"Volunteer professional" is a relatively new term.* It gives expression to the idea that, except for being unpaid, volunteers are workers who are employed, trained, supervised, promoted, dismissed, and given references as are any other

*See *The Volunteer Professional* (New York: Straus Communications, Inc., 1972), on behalf of WMCA: Call for Action.

paid staff members. Just as job descriptions and a clear statement of the terms of employment should be the norm for paid staff, so should they be available to unpaid staff — for volunteers, be they part- or full-time. Written job specifications eliminate fuzzy thinking and gray areas of responsibility in division of labor and also help to ease the threat of conflict between paid professional staff members and volunteers, discussed in the "Volunteer-to-Career" chapter of this book.

Job definitions spell out the expectations for volunteers. The benefits and rights to which volunteers are entitled by virtue of their work should also be documented. The employer's rules with regard to hiring, firing, training, supervision, and confidentiality should be clearly stated by means of a written manual or, better yet, a contract signed by both employer and employee, whether paid or not. Edna Koretsky-Warsowe, the first director of the Boston School Volunteers, maintains that "if a volunteer cannot be fired, then there had better not be a volunteer project."*

Ellen S. Straus, the founder of "Call for Action"** in New York City, an all-volunteer program which has now spread to almost fifty cities in the United States, believes that a written agreement between volunteer professionals and agencies that employ them is vital. She considers such an agreement the key to a satisfactory and lasting work experience for volunteers. It is also a safeguard for the agencies, which cannot afford to get stuck with willing but unreliable or unsuitable help — just because it comes for free.

Ms. Straus and her volunteer staff have drawn up two sets of model agreements which spell out the responsibilities, expectations, duties, and benefits of volunteers and the

*"The School Volunteer Project in Boston," in *Educational Manpower: From Aides to Differentiated Staff Patterns,* edited by James L. Olivero and Edward G. Buffie (Bloomington: Indiana University Press, 1970).

**For a detailed description of this innovative all-volunteer information and referral service using broadcasting stations and their facilities, see the end of this chapter.

employing agencies. (These model agreements are reprinted in full in the appendix.) They cover most contingencies but must, of course, be adapted to suit particular circumstances.

Such agreements are useful in many situations, although by no means in all. Particularly when dealing with loosely structured grass-roots or self-help programs, formal contracts tend to be too formidable and can be counterproductive. They may provide insufficient flexibility and stifle the very spontaneity which is such an important ingredient of volunteering.

Those utilizing any such arrangements must not lose sight of the interests and welfare of the people to be served. I am in full sympathy with the attempt to professionalize the volunteer status, but in each instance the advantages must be weighed against the danger of oppressive red tape and bureaucracy.

Reimbursement of Expenses and Proposed Tax Reforms

Ellen S. Straus and others also advocate reimbursement for expenses which a volunteer incurs, for example, transportation, lunches, and possibly child care. In some volunteer jobs, these out-of-pocket expenses can be substantial; yet few volunteers ever stop to add up the actual cost. One volunteer I know recently gave up her work simply because she could not afford to keep on shelling out money for gas, tolls, postage, film, phone calls, supplies, books, Xeroxing, as well as paying sitters for her children.

Ms. Straus had gone a giant step further by proposing tax reforms which, as an added incentive for voluntary work, would allow volunteer professionals to deduct the equivalent of the minimum wage for the job hours they put in as volunteers. Recently, Ms. Straus has changed her view regarding tax deductions; she now favors the concept of a tax *credit.* To quote from the *New York Times:*

> *[Ms. Straus's] initial proposal that volunteers be given tax deductions for their work has since been re-thought. "I feel that was an error," Ms. Straus admitted. "I am more interested in a tax credit, which would be an across-the-board kind of thing and necessary for everybody."**

Some recognition of the enormous monetary value to our society of the services freely given by volunteers is certainly in order. The details of the tax deduction proposals vary and will require further refinement. For example, NOW (the National Organization for Women) argues correctly that such a scheme should include benefits for the woman who does not serve as a volunteer for an agency but is pioneering or working independently, lobbying or doing voluntary work in the political arena.

Bills intended to implement tax-deduction proposals are already pending in Congress. They will draw strong reactions of all kinds. We must realize that, as we push for new legal rights for volunteers, we are also bound to face confrontation with existing labor-protective legislation, which may or may not be consistent with the employment of volunteer professionals. New accommodations will have to be reached. There will be controversy. That in itself is good; it helps focus attention on and interest in the novel concept of the "volunteer professional."

Insurance Benefits for Volunteers

Another recent effort to help "professionalize" volunteer employment has produced the first practical insurance for volunteers. As unpaid workers, volunteers are not covered by workmen's compensation, and traditionally they and the agencies for which they work have had inadequate liability coverage, if any. There is now a Volunteers Insurance Service

*New York Times, June 7, 1974.

Association, which has worked out a plan, with a major
insurer as underwriter, providing insurance against accident,
medical, death, and dismemberment claims on the part of
volunteers, along with liability coverage for volunteers and
employing agencies. This insurance is available in 46 states.*

In the state of Washington, at least, volunteers working for
state agencies are, since 1971, covered by the state's workmen's compensation scheme. A survey report on insurance
for volunteers has been published by the Washington State
Office of Volunteer Programs and is available upon request
from the Office of Community Development, Office of the
Governor, Olympia, Washington 98504.

Possible Social Security benefits for volunteers is another
area which needs investigating. For instance, should agencies
be permitted to make Social Security contributions on behalf
of volunteers or could volunteers become self-contributors?

"Volunteer professional" is the designation which Ellen S.
Straus would like to see women who work as volunteers list
as their occupation on drivers' licenses, passports, and
applications of all kinds, instead of the traditional "housewife."

Recently I noticed that the local newspaper had caught the
idea: the obituary of Rose B, an 82-year-old, gave her
profession as "volunteer worker," citing her 24 years of
continuous volunteer service. Little did Rose B realize that all
along in her own steady way she had been furthering the
cause of the "volunteer professional."

Portrait of a Professional Volunteer

The title may be new, but the professional volunteer has been
around for a long time. Lydia majored in English and after
graduating from college worked for four years in publishing.

*For further information contact: Corporate Insurance Management, 5301
Wisconsin Ave., N.W., Washington, D.C. 20015, or your local Voluntary Action Center.

She says matter-of-factly, "If you have actually worked, you know what work is like day in, day out — and it does not seem so glamorous." Lydia's three sons are grown, her youngest having left home nine years ago. The family has lived in the same community for 25 years.

When her children were small Lydia deliberately chose to do adult-oriented volunteer work. Her great interest in civil liberties led her to join the League of Women Voters. After a stint as president of the local chapter, she declined the offer to go on the state board. She did not want to become so busy that volunteer obligations would run her life.

Lydia starts her working day early — soon after 8 a.m. She knows herself well and admits that she needs some quiet time during the day for refueling, and it is customary in her house to "take a rest" after lunch. She and her husband participate jointly in town affairs, and eventually Lydia became secretary of the Democratic town committee and a member of the town finance committee.

Nine years ago a Democratic governor appointed her to the Board of Library Commissioners, and her term was renewed by the succeeding Republican governor. She has served as chairwoman of the board for the past four years. This unpaid lay board is the policy-making arm of the state-level library agency. As such, the board is responsible for state and federal library programs, including school library aid; library facilities for the blind, the handicapped, and in-state institutions; the regional public library systems; and the certification of librarians. With responsibility for the funds, the service, and the leadership role in this agency, Lydia feels that she has more power as a volunteer than any paid position would offer her at this stage of her life.

Lydia's third major concern is ecology. She was instrumental in starting the Charles River Valley Group of the League of Women Voters, a consortium of the 21 leagues in the Charles River Watershed Association. This has been an education-

and-action group and has led Lydia to edit four editions of a booklet, give slide talks, take groups on tours, confer with officials, and work with other volunteers. Many of the women originally involved in the group have themselves ranged out in allied concerns — they have become members of conservation commissions, leaders of the Charles River Watershed Association, or they have branched out into other fields such as "solid waste" or air pollution — and there is serious consideration being given to disbanding the group. One volunteer suggested that every organization should "have a self-destruct button" and be wise enough to use it at the appropriate time so as not to outlive its usefulness.

Lydia says she has applied all of her previous training — her writing skills, her photography, her experience in the publishing trade — in her volunteer work.

In all of these years she has never been tempted to look for a paid career position, and none has been offered her which would have been as interesting and as wide-ranging as her volunteer jobs. Lydia discovered to her intense pleasure at a recent family reunion how proudly her sons speak of their mother's active concerns.

Lydia has found that it does not take long to become knowledgeable in almost any field which engages one's genuine interest. She says:

> *You must be sufficiently articulate so that the experts and decision makers will take you seriously. It is important to do one's homework. In addition, a woman has a little extra advantage — that spare hour to go and take a look for herself. For instance, if a new source of river pollution is discovered or a wetland is in danger of being filled, I have the time to go and see for myself, photograph the scene, and talk to officials. If testimony for a bill or project is needed, I have the flexibility to lobby at the State House (which I have often done), or even at the Congress in Washington.*

Lydia is not stigmatized as an "amateur." Being both tactful and sensitive, she has been able to work with all kinds of experts without making them feel insecure or impatient. Lydia's husband has given her solid backing all these years. (She does adjust her vacation schedule to his whenever possible.)

Somewhere along the line she also fits in a four-hour stint each week as a "Call-for-Action" volunteer at a local radio station. Lydia has always worked as one of a group and has not experienced the loneliness that an individual crusader sometimes suffers. When the fight seems uphill all the way, there are good friends and like-minded volunteer colleagues to help keep her going.

Obviously Lydia has given a great deal of consideration to both the caliber of her work as a volunteer and its effects on her personal life and family lifestyle. She successfully maintains that "delicate balance" between the two which many other women search for.

Lydia hopes very much to do some "oral history" after her term on the Library Extension Board expires. And, she says, she is saving some unpopular causes for her old age! Not everyone can or should be as high-powered a volunteer as Lydia, but her serious commitment to a volunteer task is worth imitating.

Example of One Active Volunteer Program Staffed
by Volunteer Professionals

Call for Action is a telephone information and referral service. With the participation of leading radio stations in more than fifty cities throughout the United States, it is one of the latest and most imaginative volunteer programs operating on a national level.

Staffed entirely by volunteers, and backed by the "clout" of the media, CFA is remarkably effective in cutting through the complexities of contemporary urban living. Volunteers refer inquiries in a myriad of categories to the proper federal, state,

municipal, or private agencies. All calls are confidential.

The program has a twofold purpose: first, to service the callers; and, second, on a long-range basis, to use the information gathered by the calls and consequent experiences with the agencies to work toward institutional change.

In Boston, Call for Action was started in 1970. Five phone lines are open Monday through Friday, from 11 a.m. to 1 p.m. The highly trained volunteer staff gives information and offers referrals. Two weeks after the original contact, Call for Action volunteers check to see whether the client has been helped. If not, other referrals are suggested, or, as in about twenty percent of the cases, Call for Action acts as ombudsman, prodding the agencies and researching community facilities.

Approximately fifty Call for Action volunteers work at WBZ in Boston. Preceding the opening of the service, the team of volunteer supervisors put together a referral directory (a labor of love which took almost a full year to complete). This directory, on a Rollex system, contains detailed information on more than 1,200 federal, state, and city departments, private agencies and organizations throughout the Boston metropolitan area. Wherever possible personal working contacts have been established. This directory, an indispensable tool, is constantly being updated, a challenging and never-ending volunteer task in itself.

In its first full year of operation WBZ Call for Action received more than 12,000 calls. CFA tries to improve community facilities and services through radio editorials, through letters to officials or to "The Editor," and through testimony on their findings before Massachusetts legislative committees.

Boston's WBZ-CFA has had a very low rate of staff turnover. Volunteers may work exclusively on the phones or on editorial ideas, do research or public relations, or prepare and present testimony. Many opt for more than one phase of the program.

The CFA office is crowded, and the atmosphere is friendly and without protocol. Nevertheless, volunteers are given a thorough training and are held to a high standard of performance. After a day on the phones volunteers inevitably feel they have learned something new and have helped someone toward the solution of a bewildering or frustrating problem.

PART TWO

Who Volunteers?

Dedicated to the memory of a greatly missed friend,

ELI GOLDSTON

who knew much about work
who was learning about the changing roles of women,
and who himself was a volunteer par excellence.

7

The High School Student

Not all volunteers go the route of the "volunteer professional": people can and should choose volunteer work most suitable to their particular circumstances.

Students, whose flexible schedules easily lend themselves to volunteer activity during the summer, school year, or while on leave, find in volunteering a way to supplement their formal education. Mothers, aware that family responsibilities need not preclude community service, may use part-time volunteering to maintain contact with the outside world and to avoid becoming isolated from social issues or cut off from previous professional interests. Women alone, whether they be single, widowed, or divorced, volunteer to integrate themselves better into the community, as well as for other reasons. Retirees, instead of feeling rejected, may experience a new surge of life by giving service to others.

Leaves of Absence: the Term Off

Educators and parents alike have long realized that summer vacations offer the possibility of expanding education beyond the classroom; they accept camps, traveling, special study and arts programs, or practical work experience as legitimate summer activities for their children.*

However, some of today's students, troubled by a variety of

---

*The Parents League of Greater Boston publishes a well-researched manual, *Summer Opportunities for Young People,* edited by Gernda Neuhauser. It describes a wide range of options, including both "traditional" and community-service-oriented activities.

social issues and faced with a scarcity of paid jobs, use summer vacations as a first opportunity to participate in volunteer community service. For many, this brief exposure to the "real" world is so rewarding that they choose to take a more extended leave from formal schooling.

Each year more young people seek this alternative to the lockstep of twelve, sixteen, or more continuous years of schooling. They feel the need for a break in their classroom studies. The stretch from kindergarten through grade school, from high school to college, and then perhaps on to graduate work need no longer be an uninterrupted process of learning within the confines of four walls. As John Bremer, former director of the Parkway Program in Philadelphia, put it:

> *Learning is not something that goes on only in special places called classrooms, or in special buildings called schools. It is a quality of life appropriate to any and every phase of human existence . . . it is human life itself.*

Sonja, English teacher and advisor to the senior class at a school in Cambridge, writes:

> *At a time when many high schools are releasing their seniors ahead of time to solve — or to avoid — the problems of "Senior Slump," our school has chosen an entirely different course. Instead of "no school" or "school that doesn't really count" we have offered a program of seminars, senior projects, and research papers. In other words, we have offered the seniors a chance to do more rather than less.*

These students are well prepared academically, they have taken innumerable exams, their college applications are completed, and they want to try their wings. Sonja sums it up well: "They are not in college yet, but they want to live and work as if they were. This mid-year break — not June — is the real division between secondary school and college."

Here is one school which has shown itself to be both sensitive and resourceful in its response to its students' pleas for more involvement in the outside world. The seniors play a part in shaping the curriculum, and the independent activity is entirely an individual choice. The majority of girls and boys choose to work as volunteers in the community.

Last year, for her senior project, Ann worked as a nurse's aide in the intensive care unit of a local hospital, making beds, bathing, feeding, and talking to patients, keeping a detailed diary all the while. The following are some entries from Ann's diary which speak for themselves:

Assignment: Working in the Intensive Care Unit from 9:00 to 12:00 and in the X-ray Department until 2:00.

I woke up this morning to the alarm, got dressed in a comfortable dress, and started on my 15-minute walk to the hospital. After getting lost among the corridors, I found Mrs. J, the Director of Volunteers. She seemed very anxious to have me, and we discussed what my job would consist of: working in the X-ray office, typing, filing, and arranging X-rays. I told Mrs. J that I wanted to do something that would give me a real dose of hospital life as I was thinking of becoming a nurse. She started to describe a job that sounded really challenging, but scary at that particular moment. It would be working in the intensive care unit. We discussed everything — the trials of the work, the walking, the importance of paying attention at all times, of staying out of the way in emergencies, of reporting fire drills, where to report in case of an emergency, such as a plane crash or fire. She gave me a booklet on do's and don't's of intensive care, on general behavior, and on details of work.

Within the first week Ann writes:

I worked on the second floor with two volunteers, giving out water and liquids. It was quite enjoyable. I was taken on a two-hour tour of the hospital showing me how to perform different duties that I would be responsible for. I was shown how to take different specimens to different places, how to get blood for transfusion purposes from where, how to stamp different slips for the lab, and for the pharmacy, and where the different departments were (EKG [electrocardiogram] diagnosis, storeroom, pharmacy, lab, switchboard, medical records, X-rays, etc.).

Then a few days later:

Today my job was totally different from what I had expected. I felt as though I were a registered nurse with all the immediate action. A nurse and I helped to lift a very old, very sick woman from a stretcher to the X-ray table. She had tubes running through her nose, and she had a tube leading into a bowl filled with milky white urine from her kidneys. The nurse had disconnected the tube and the urine was all over the woman — her chest, her hair, her johnny robe, and the table. I was shocked and mildly repulsed. I had thought I would faint at the sight of anything along that line. I felt very sorry for her, and I couldn't see how the nurses could throw her around the way they did. They struck me as very hardened people. I vowed then that I would never forget that every patient has feelings of pain. After she finished with her X-rays, we wheeled her back to intensive care.

After the X-ray scene which I thought had prepared me for all my days at the hospital, I went to the blood bank to get some blood for transfusion purposes; delivered mail; fetched water; stamped pharmaceutical and X-ray slips; picked up drugs for patients; and made up a stretcher. When the day was over I realized that I would be able to hold myself together and function in emergencies (the X-ray was an emergency at this point).

Then during the second week on hospital volunteer duty:

Today I started out by giving patients fresh water

*and by changing their paper bags. My hands were shaking. I am so
scared I will do something wrong and cause a heart attack or
something. The patients seem so weak and helpless; some of them
cannot even speak or move. What would happen if I tripped over an
intravenous tube or spilled water all over them? One man was having
heart problems. I left early because I had a headache. I notice that I
become very flushed and nervous when I am with the patients. I guess I
am not used to the atmosphere yet.*

*Everyone at the hospital seems very cheery. It is as though they
really belong there. I don't feel that way as yet. I am pretty much alone
now. I sometimes get the sense that everybody knows exactly what
they are doing and knows everyone else.*

*I can't help wondering what the patients are suffering from. Some of
them enjoy talking about what is wrong with them but I don't think I
should pry.*

Slowly she begins to become somewhat used to the routine
and records:

*I was very disappointed to find that I had such
limits put on my activities, though. Everything I did, from feeding a
patient, lifting or lowering a bed, administering water (straw? cup?),
removing a bedpan, and removing a food tray had to be OK'd by the
nurse. I began to realize, however,* that what I was there for, was
not to take away each nurse's duties, but to make things easier
for the nurses and the patients. *I found that this was the most
rewarding approach.*

Then weeks later Ann is able to say:

*After a while I learned to recognize what could be
done to certain patients without consulting the nurse.*

*For the first couple of weeks, before I really had command of the
situation, I left the hospital with a feeling of "what am I doing here?" I
had begun to really enjoy the work, but I always had a feeling of
wanting to do more, to know more, and be of some valuable assistance
as an authority. I never knew what all the diagnoses were and always*

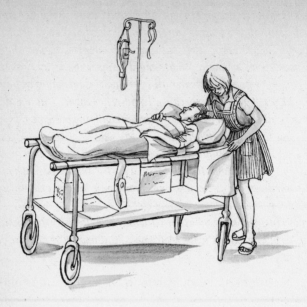

was in a state of curiosity.

On May 1st I was introduced to X-ray transporting and that was the actual turning point in my work. The people working there are a lot friendlier than the nurses on Ward 3A. Transporting patients is really thrilling for me. I get to ride the elevator a lot and chat with all the people leaving and entering the hospital.

Mrs. S is ninety years old and senile. All the patients from the 3B Ward used to complain about her wailing. Guess who had to wheel her down to X-ray? A boy from X-ray helped me do it. It was one of the most frightening things I've ever been through. She screamed and screamed at anything. She looked so fragile I thought she would crack any minute.

Then a few days later, Ann helped with an emergency case, a woman with a ruptured gall bladder. She writes:

It was the first time that I had ever seen a nurse so grateful for my help. I really felt that I had accomplished something.

Toward the end of her term:

> *I trained three women to work in intensive care next fall. It was probably more educational for me than for them, because* I learned how not to be a bad volunteer. *My first trainee walked through the corridors as though she owned the place. She went barging into all the rooms, whether there was a doctor, visitor, or what. I told her to go in only when the curtains were open. She insisted that if she were going to volunteer, the doctors would be glad to have her any time. I told her that the best approach would be to be on the meek side, to let the doctor finish his examination and work in another room meanwhile. She seemed to think her time was too valuable, and that the hospital was lucky to have her!*

The following is Ann's summary of her experience of a "term off":

> *My project was a success. It started out on the slow side but has reached a climax. I am going to work until the end of June and have been offered a Saturday job in the X-ray department. Because of this project I* really *consider becoming a nurse or a doctor.*

Ann tasted a slice of life, worried, and agonized, but found that she could cope. She did outstanding work and was offered a paid summer job, and she may even have found out that she would enjoy the life of a doctor or nurse.

Not every student has such a successful term off. Some decide, as a result of their volunteer experience, that they are not interested in a particular field. Betty got a volunteer apprenticeship in an urban-redevelopment office. Interested in architecture and city planning, she found that her job was more tedious than she had expected; she spent hours building models for inner-city housing projects. This kind of occupation, where one slip of the knife can ruin weeks of work, requires extreme patience and care and was not at all right for her.

Bad experience with those people responsible for volunteer

projects often proves counterproductive. For their term-off activity, a group of high school students wanted to work on physical rehabilitation of houses. When they showed up for the job, there were no materials or tools, and the tenants did not even know they were coming. Despite their best efforts to convince their supervisor that they could make a significant improvement in the dilapidated housing, the volunteers were continually frustrated by sloppy management and poor planning. After several weeks of vain attempts, they became disgusted and gave up.

Finally, one very bright girl decided to use her term off to do paralegal work for a legal aid society. Without any previous legal training, Laura was doing a better job at counseling clients than some members of the staff. In legal aid work, sympathetic listening and counseling may often be as valuable as technical advice. Some of the professionals began to feel threatened by the ease with which Laura related to their clients. When too many applicants specifically requested appointments with Laura, she was asked to leave the office.

On the whole, however, students report very rewarding experiences. One of Ann's classmates made children's toys for the educational television station. Liz worked at the state's fish and game department. Yet another fish fancier designed and built an aquarium for the younger children at her school.

Three other girls in that class obtained paid summer jobs as a result of their independent projects, one of them designing and sewing costumes for a Shakespearean performance, the two others teaching younger children. Julie's term off in her senior year will lead to a year off before college. Her volunteer work at a Montessori school has turned into a full-time paid job.

It seems that independent schools have pioneered the way, and the concept of the "term off" has become an accepted way of life at many of them. Public schools are beginning to follow suit.

One of several new educational programs in metropolitan Boston, set up to meet the need for a structured term off program for seniors in public high schools, is the Independent Study Project which began operating in the fall of 1971. This cooperative educational experiment is co-sponsored by two nonprofit agencies and is jointly funded. Nine public schools were picked to participate in the Independent Study Project for a social, geographical, ethnic, and racial balance. Boston English and the Jeremiah Burke schools are inner-city schools and 80 percent black. Boston Latin is the intellectually elite school for boys (now admitting girls, also), while the students at Brighton and Somerville high schools are from predominantly white working-class families. Wellesley High represents a wealthy suburb with a tradition of innovative education. The participation and intermingling of students from urban and suburban schools lends the ISP a special flavor and makes it unique in Boston. Over 150 internships were lined up in advance during the summer and fall, and contracts were signed with the participating organizations or businesses. The program was explained to school superintendents, principals, guidance counselors, and students from the designated schools. Counselors met with the students individually and in groups and matched student requests to the available internships. Employers provided on-the-job training and guidance. The students may work several hours a week to full time during the last half of their senior year. Producing a taped slide show as well as a 30-minute TV show the educational television network did much to keep the students interested and involved throughout the entire period. Out of 95 students enrolled in the program in 1971, 87 completed their internships and would enroll again if given the chance. Ninety-five percent of the organizations and firms who took part in the first year asked for interns for the following year.

In subsequent discussions and written evaluations, the student interns have pointed out that the following are vital to the success of the project: enough released time from school work, ease of transportation, sufficient funds for travel, strong motivation, interesting internships, good supervision, enough school credits, and good follow-through by all parties concerned.

As an experiment in educational change the Independent Study Project fits into the new concept of the "flexible" or "open" campus plan which originated in Philadelphia. It is based on the conviction that in the future education must be the function of the total community, and that citizens should once again join educators in the teaching of their children. The project encourages the close cooperation of students, educators, and civic and business representatives.

It is often left up to the students to make arrangements for "meaningful work" while on leave of absence from school. Making these arrangements for oneself can be a major part of the learning experience. Yet, with so many work-term students flooding the market, it is becoming much harder to find interesting assignments. Some schools assign teachers and counselors to assist with this task; frequently they have to learn along with the students seeking placement. The resources of a big city seem unlimited, but competent persons to supervise the troops of eager yet untrained volunteers are at a premium. Supervision takes time and energy, and the return for the organization or business is not always immediate. Mel Miller, editor of the *Bay State Banner*, a daily newspaper for the black community in Boston, estimates that it takes from four to six weeks before a volunteer apprentice becomes useful to his operation. While expecting any volunteer to perform much of the dull routine work involved in putting out a daily paper, he is very realistic about the investment of time and energy his staff must make to really bring along a student volunteer. For that reason Mel Miller likes to see his successful volunteer interns continue throughout the summer, which is easily arranged when the spring term is chosen for work away from school. Frequently, therefore, the "term off" turns into six months of volunteer on-the-job training.

Occasionally there is a stipend for summer work. Paid summer jobs for students are in very short supply at the present time. The volunteer who has done a good job during spring term often has first option on any paid position that opens up within the organization he or she has worked for.

Leaves of Absence: The Year Off

Not so many years ago, it was considered most unorthodox for a student to take an entire year off before college and was allowed only for "special cases." To say that the practice of interrupting one's academic career is becoming standard operating procedure may still be too sweeping a generalization; yet it would seem that this trend is only another of the many changes taking place in education across the country. After experiencing unusually large numbers of dropouts among some of the ablest and most promising students, often from college freshman classes, educators have been taking a long hard look at the underlying causes and have come up with some practical solutions. It is possible to discern a pattern, among school guidance counselors and university admissions officers, of encouraging students who have doubts about a college career to take a year off between high school and college. One response to the problem manifests itself in the growing number of colleges which will accept students with the option of postponing actual entrance by twelve months and guarantee them a place in the class the following year.

It is clear that students wishing to take a full year off may avail themselves of many of the same options already described. But the longer period, an entire year as opposed to one term, permits students to participate in more structured programs if they so choose; more and more it seems that volunteer service provides an acceptable alternative.

One Alternative for a Structured "Year Off"

The Dynamy Program in Worcester, Massachusetts, and in St. Paul, Minnesota, was developed to attract young people who would like to test out classroom theories in the real world of public affairs and business. Here, young women and men between the ages of sixteen and twenty find a carefully structured nine months of work and learning, which provides them with a diverse sequence of personal experience in a supportive enviroment. They are challenged to develop creative problem-solving abilities in real-life situations rather than in academic exercises. Dynamy tries to achieve these goals by offering a series of internships in various areas of community service, and supplements them with other activities such as seminars, field trips, retreats, and an orientation period including three weeks of Outward Bound-type training. As the catalog states, "There are no specific academic prerequisities for participation in Dynamy. Some interns may have completed a year or two of college; some may not have finished high school."

Because of its structure, its residential facilities for students, and its generous staff-student ratio, Dynamy is of necessity an expensive program to operate. Even though some scholarships are available, the program must rely largely on a fee-paying clientele.

A Year of Realistic Pre-vocational Options

Another experimental program for adolescents stresses the need for effective pre-vocational exploration. Here is a partial description of its philosophy from the Tunbridge catalog:

A major aspect of entering adulthood is the choice of one's work. Work will of necessity absorb much of each individual's life, in many cases providing a major source of satisfaction and meaning. With minor exceptions there is no provision in the education of the young to permit them wide-ranging realistic pre-vocational exploration. *In cart-before-horse fashion, students are called upon to make vocational decisions first, and only then are they given exposure to the field. Most training is done in school environments which present a distorted, or at least a limited, picture of what work in a given field is like. The social aspects of work are as important to individuals as the mechanical ones. What is needed are arrangements which will permit students to explore virtually any field in its actual setting and in ways which will provide an introduction which is condensed without being misleading or superficial. Such an introduction must also provide an opportunity for doing as well as observing, and this without requiring prolonged training.*

Again, very high fees put this program out of reach for the average young person and, in fact, hastened its demise.

Other Alternatives for High School Students

For the public school system, a program like Dynamy can serve as a model for alternative education. Eugene J. Applebaum, the supervisor of program development for Worcester's city schools, hopes that "within a matter of a couple of years at the most, we should see elements of Dynamy existing in all of our schools. The internships certainly will." In fact they do exist in a growing number of public schools even now. Mr. Applebaum goes on to say that "with the cost of education rising . . . we will use more community leaders as teachers and more blocks of time for more students to be working in the community." But he also warns (and I am in complete agreement with him) that there is a saturation point and that alternative school patterns will not replace more traditional school curricula. Alternative schools do make possible genuine choices of learning styles. And that, it seems to me, is what the 1970s are all about: the introduction of a great number of choices in lifestyles, education, and work patterns for individuals of all ages and both sexes.

It is perhaps still too early to evaluate the results of high school students' involvement in organized volunteer programs. Many of the independent study programs, internships, and experimental student programs mentioned here are only now gaining true nationwide acceptance. Although I recognize the extreme difficulty of assessing the intangibles of the volunteer experience, results from the current "Study of Programs of Off-Campus Education for Secondary School Students"* should provide interesting data. While off-campus education in the form of voluntary community service should not replace an academic education, in today's world it is undoubtedly a necessary complement. To deny this aspect of education would be to deprive young people of an important potential for growth.

*Under the auspices of the National Association of Independent Schools, directed by Alan R. Blackmer. Funds for this study were provided by the Breitmayer Foundation.

8

The Undergraduate

When the college student decides to volunteer, he or she is likely to have more complex reasons to do so than a younger brother or sister would have. At the college level the motivation for getting involved in volunteer work varies much more from person to person and is often connected with the search for career goals.

Learning, personal growth, and establishing one's identity are what the college years are all about. Working in the "real" world makes an important contribution to that growth experience. Juniors and, particularly, seniors are looking ahead with some trepidation to what comes next, what comes after college. Some feel obvious relief at the prospect of ending years of formal education. But career decisions must now be faced, and the "real" world looms rather large.

Often the prospective college graduate has no clearer idea of vocational goals than he or she had at the time of entering college. A survey of 94 percent of the 1,439 members of the joint Harvard and Radcliffe class of 1972 showed that at the time of graduation three out of ten men and one out of five women were uncertain as to what their eventual vocations would be. An unprecedentedly high proportion of 31 percent of men and 41 percent of women were looking for short-term work, unrelated to any career goal. Of the job-seeking

Radcliffe graduates, 68 percent were still jobless at the time of
the survey.

The Reverend Robert J. Ginn, Jr., co-author of the survey
report, cites volunteer term-time experience as the "single
most important activity in contributing to a therapeutic
resolution of the crisis of indecision." Ginn asserts that
indecision is an inevitable by-product of liberal arts curricula
and can be effectively resolved only through the commitment
of university faculty and administrators to the idea that
volunteer activity "is vital to the students' social and
intellectual growth." He argues further that volunteer work
isolated from faculty evaluation and support, isolated from
the classroom experience, lacks the "emotional potency" of
volunteer programs which are strongly supported by faculty
who "consider volunteering an activity central to the
educational experience of each student."

This report also strongly recommends that in order to
overcome career indecision, universities should give more
support to students' leaves-of-absence and should provide
more assistance in locating useful term-time experience, on
either a paid or *volunteer* basis.

Uncertainty about career plans is due in part to a lack of or
confusing overabundance of options and to the inability to
define goals and relate them to the job opportunities.
According to a George Gallup poll, one third of all the young
people in the 18-29 age bracket, working in the United States,
don't like their jobs. They admit freely that they loaf on jobs
which provide them money but no satisfaction.* Hence it is
not surprising that some of our most thoughtful young people
are reluctant to follow the traditional ways of entering the
work world.

I agree with Ginn in his estimation of the importance of
volunteer work in overcoming career uncertainty. But, in

*George Gallup, Jr., at a seminar of the American Management Association.

addition, at the undergraduate stage volunteer work also
meets the need of many students to break out of the ivory
tower, to become involved in real life problems while
continuing academic studies, or simply to help others.
Volunteering can be part of course work or quite separate
from it.

Volunteering to Test Interests and Abilities

Juliet, a college senior, is still uncertain about a
career, and volunteering is helping her to clarify her
vocational questions. Juliet's mother, a historian, died during
Juliet's freshman year. Some day Juliet may want to carry on
some of the work her mother left unfinished, but for the
moment she is concerned that she may not be able to live up to
her mother's standards and is looking for ways to test her
own strengths. Juliet confirms that "for me, volunteering
while at college has been a way of discovering what I might
like to do professionally, what I can do, feel comfortable
doing, and am good at." She considers volunteering as a link
with the world outside college. As a consequence she may try
out a job in social service.

Juliet's reaction warrants a closer look at her volunteer
work. This year it is course-connected. She spends two half
days a week at a pregnancy counseling service as part of the
field work for a social relations course concerned with social
change and its inherent stresses. Her course paper based on
this experience illustrates the scope of the learning experience
offered by well-run agencies to a responsible volunteer, as
well as the depth of understanding she gained in the process.
After describing the agency's objectives and operations, she
observes that its principal role appears to be that of a "talking
cure," which in Juliet's words "emphasizes reducing fear and
anxiety by providing accurate information on abortion or
adoption procedures or benefits to unwed mothers, and
letting the client come to her own decision, without feeling

pressured in any one direction." She notes with approval that the agency's counselors "adjust the treatment to the client's needs rather than the reverse." The fact that volunteers constitute almost the entire counseling staff has led her to deduce that the agency's administrators believe that "the problem of women with unwanted pregnancies can be dealt with by a trained volunteer staff"; also, that the supervisors place more value on suitability and experience than on credentials. Her evaluation of the counselors is very positive, and she perceives the dangers of judgmental responses and overidentification.

Her understanding of the agency's objectives is best demonstrated by her criticism and suggestions. She questions the inadequacy of the effort to reach the low-income women who need pregnancy counseling services the most. Aware of the financial limitations of the agency, she nevertheless suggests introducing baby-sitting and free transportation, which might encourage such women to come for help. She also deplores an important unsolved problem, the lack of effective post-abortion counseling.

All of this is based on Juliet's work in a clerical capacity only. When she wrote the paper she had not even begun her training for the actual work of pregnancy counseling. Yet the agency provided the kind of orientation, supervision, and opportunity to explore and question which enabled her to understand in considerable depth how the agency works, why, and to what extent it accomplishes its purposes. This speaks well for the agency, and to me it spells true *volunteer participation* as opposed to mere *utilization of volunteers*.

And most important, through the accompanying course work Juliet has been able to avail herself of intellectual and philosophical support. Her professor's comments on her outstanding paper and his interest in her top quality work in that field lent much added weight to the volunteer phase of Juliet's senior year at college.

Course-Connected Volunteering

Many college courses today require or allow field work for which course credit is given, and, as in Juliet's case, volunteer work in the community often is accepted for this purpose. But the premise is a controversial one.

As recently as 1967 Hilda Hubbell* wrote in *Women's Education* that "there is little or no evidence of preparation of students in undergraduate or graduate schools for working as and with volunteers." The "with" refers to the time in the future when the students themselves have become trained professionals and will be in a position to help strengthen the roles volunteers can play.**

One of the major points in Harvard President Derek Bok's speech of September 1972, mentioned earlier, was his admonition to the incoming class "to devote [their] talents and energies in generous measure to the problems and welfare of others." He went on to say that "students are showing an active concern over a variety of ethical and social issues during their college careers . . . with more activity, more debate, and more protest about moral problems than most of us can remember." Yet he, too, conceded that the colleges themselves have still not done enough to help.

I agree on both counts. Even though "our colleges and universities do not yet include in their curricula a freshman orientation course in community service as a requirement for graduation," as suggested by Mrs. Hubbell, much progress has been made since 1967. But we cannot afford to rest on these laurels. Not only could the colleges do much more in this regard, but I sense they are in very real danger of backsliding.

Many of the changes have come in response to the tumultuous years of student strikes and unrest of the sixties. If there is a cooling of student interest in community involve-

*Director of Volunteer Services at the Health and Welfare Council of the National Capital Area.

**See in this connection Chapter 12, "The Volunteer-to-Career Concept."

ment (as, unfortunately, there seems to be), college and university administrators might well respond, under financial and other pressures, by allowing such programs to die. This would be a very unfortunate misinterpretation of what is happening to the students and to the world around us.

Whatever may be the factors that make for a more quiescent student body at this time, the need to supplement academic study in many fields with community action experience is as great as ever. We have learned that the gap between alienated students and effective community action is harder to traverse than most students and program administrators thought. Indeed, such community action programs, because they deal with actual people and life situations, tend to shock students into comprehending the seriousness of that gap and how hard it will be to fulfill their expectation of finding some undefined exotic, independent career after graduation. The resulting frustration may be the reason for any current reduction in student pressures for community action.

I suggest, therefore, that this is a time for perseverance by university administrators — a time of challenge to their leadership qualities. As the rest of this chapter — and I hope, much of this book — demonstrates, when universities offer imaginative programs, there are ample takers. Therefore, the response to reduced student agitation must be to increase and improve such programs — not to curtail them. Administrators began by responding to student-created emergencies. I hope they will now take the opportunity to innovate and lead, not simply in order to forestall new emergencies, but also because it is educationally and socially sound to continue in these new directions.

The benefits of a "practicum" by students are widely recognized. The controversy tends to be not about the usefulness of community-type field work as an adjunct to appropriate courses, but rather about the extent to which such work should be considered part and parcel of the course and

therefore entitled to credit. There has been much discussion but little agreement about where to fix the point at which "pay" for such work (be it academic credit or even a subsistence allowance) stops it from being "volunteer" work. During the past decade Peace Corps and VISTA volunteers have had to come to terms with similar questions.

To me, this line of reasoning misses the main point. Neither course credit nor pocket money precludes the mutual give-and-take that is the key to constructive community work. Nor does the absence of credit or financial remuneration assure this give-and-take. For example, a woman who volunteers merely in order to get out of the house, without any real concern for the work she does as a volunteer, really belongs in the "pay" category. She does it almost exclusively for what she can get out of it, though no credit is given and no money changes hands. On the other hand, the student who earns credit and perhaps some pocket money, but who is committed and cares, and gives freely — talents, time, and emotions — is a constructive volunteer. Whether technically he or she should be labeled a "volunteer" or rather an "intern" seems to me of secondary importance. I do recognize, of course, that there is a point where payment becomes so significant that "volunteering" becomes a misnomer.

The reason that money has entered this discussion at all is that there are now programs in which cash is offered as part of the incentive for volunteering. The controversial University Year of Action program, for example, funded by the federal government, often works that way. University Year of Action is under the jurisdiction of ACTION, the federal agency now also in charge of the Peace Corps, VISTA, and other volunteer projects. It offers funds to universities for the administration of community-action programs which use university resources. Participating students must commit themselves to a year of full-time community work in poverty areas. They get college credit for this year and may be paid a living allowance averaging $200 per month. There are currently more than 1,000 such students at 24 colleges across the country and the number is growing.

Gaining a full year's academic credit for community action work is very desirable to some students, who prefer to function in the world of action rather than in the library and the classroom. Such programs can unquestionably be valid educational experiences entitled to credit if, and this is a big "if," there is tight, competent, and demanding faculty supervision.

But we must also recognize that when the incentives are so rich, involving both academic credit and money, the risk becomes very great that the "gain-a-year" motive totally obliterates the "give-a-year" objective. Only the future will tell whether programs offering such relatively heavy material rewards can succeed on a broad scale.

There is danger of "cheap" academic credits being obtained for work which is not significant or sufficiently demanding educationally in the field where credit is sought. Furthermore, only a limited number of professors themselves have first-hand experience in community work. There is a tendency to be too theoretical. And unlike the professors of the social relations course which Juliet attends (and which I audited) many of the teachers are not qualified to help their students integrate their field experience with their academic studies.

As such programs grow and the number of interested students increases, I foresee a serious lack of supervisory staff, at the agencies as well as among the university faculties. This is bound to have a critical effect on the success of such programs — both for the participating students and for the recipients of their proffered services.

Yet neither of these risks in any way contradicts the basic need: that more be done to relate academic learning to its practical use and application. Nor does it negate the conclusion that volunteer community action is a useful and mutually productive tool to those ends. How much academic credit should be given for such work, and how teachers should be trained to integrate it into the curriculum are side issues, important though they are.

Despite concerns over programs such as University Year of Action, there is no doubt that they are helping many students bridge the perceived gap between taught knowledge and knowledge gained from experience. To take an example: one University of Massachusetts UYA student had the opportunity, as part of her volunteer assignment with the Massachusetts Law Reform Institute, to help prepare a legislative proposal that would abolish Massachusetts' ancient "stubborn child" laws. These laws make truancy and stubbornness crimes for minors (when these laws were first adopted in 1649, they included the death penalty for disobedient boys!). The proposed law would substitute a broad new civil category of "children in need of services." The resulting bill, introduced in the state legislature, has just recently been adopted. Such volunteer participation in real-life lawmaking is, of course, an ideal way to bring course work alive.

Volunteering Outside Course Work

Students engaged in volunteer work long before there was any thought of course credit or government-financed encouragement. And they continue to do so. The opportunities for such work are at least as great and varied as those I have described for nonstudent adults. Many organizations are interested in a mixture of volunteers of all ages and backgrounds, and students often bring a youthful enthusiasm and a fresh point of view to the work that needs to be done. In addition, there are innumerable student-run volunteer efforts.

Many students find their volunteer jobs independently or through friends, advertisements, or clearinghouses in the community. The larger universities have their own volunteer clearinghouses, which maintain listings of volunteer opportunities; prospective student volunteers can get guidance and advice there. Most universities have a number of group projects, run and staffed by students with or without faculty supervision. These students tend to specialize in specific areas of social concern and, as in the case of Radcliffe's "Education-for-Action" program, are entirely committed to working for social change.

Only a few universities employ paid coordinators for their student volunteer clearinghouses. Frequently universities ask their student employment officers to do volunteer placement counseling along with their other duties.

As I mentioned in the beginning of this chapter, the search for career goals is an important motivation for undergraduates who volunteer. That is the broad objective. For some students, volunteering helps test out the solidity and seriousness of a perceived special interest. For others, volunteering is a way to confirm or deny a gnawing suspicion that they are in the wrong field, that another field may hold promise of greater success and satisfaction. The variations on the central theme of wanting and needing to test possible interests and abilities are endless.

And last but by no means least, let us not forget that with all these purposeful approaches to volunteering, many students do it just for fun and personal satisfaction.

It is hoped that the following cases, describing actual experiences by student volunteers, speak for themselves:

Volunteering to Pursue a Special Interest. Liz chose her university in part for its outstanding volunteer center; she even selected her major, social relations, with these active outside interests in mind. Except for some tutoring she had had no previous volunteer experience in the affluent Chicago suburb where she grew up. Once at the university, she started her volunteer work career in mental health; but when an opportunity arose to team up with a graduate student to co-teach a psychology course at a large state prison, she took it. Over the next couple of years she discovered that she relates well to the prisoners, likes to teach them, and is successful at it. Eventually she was given sole responsibility for the course. Now in her senior year, she has been elected head of the Prisons Reform Committee. Working with well over a hundred student members, all of them volunteering in prisons, is quite a large administrative job.

Liz is quick to point out that the volunteer work she observes is not necessarily altruistic — that a majority of the students do it as much, if not more, for themselves, to test their abilities and interests and to learn more about the world outside academia. She feels that in the last few years women as well as men have been forced to depend more upon themselves, on their own strengths and skills, other relationships not providing the kind of support they did before. Liz is on her way to becoming an effective worker for social change.

Volunteering to Test an Intended Change of Field of Concentration. Charlotte really wanted to study early childhood development at a small teachers' training college, but her parents — themselves involved in the publishing world — had different ideas for her and strongly urged her to go to a large university and major in fine arts. Charlotte followed their wishes, but was extremely unhappy with the choice. She was able to convince her parents to let her drop out of the university if she could show them that she had an acceptable alternative plan.

At that stage Charlotte appeared at our volunteer counseling service and, after looking into several placements suggested to her, decided to work in one of the city's elementary schools as a school volunteer. Charlotte was very fortunate to be assigned to an inspired and dedicated teacher who recognized her talents and was eager to train and supervise her.

Through her volunteer work, Charlotte was able to prove to herself and to her family that teaching really was her first love and that she had a natural gift for it. She then reapplied to and was accepted by the college of her original choice and has since graduated. She is now a full-time teacher herself, assisted by a school volunteer.

Volunteering for the Fun of It. Donna, a drama student, has learned the business of dog-clipping during her high school summer vacations. She must earn money for her

personal expenses and does so by working for a pet and grooming service. Donna feels that with her limited spare time she can make the most effective contribution by volunteering her rather unusual and specialized skills. Animal shelters turn to her for help with any stray dogs who need clipping care, as well as tick and flea baths. She does it for free, of course. Her only problem is to keep the flow of "clipping scholarships" for lost pets at a manageable rate.

A Case That Sums It All Up. Andrea is 27 years old and a student placement officer at the University of Massachusetts. Her description of her own volunteer experiences and her evolving philosophy pulls together the various strands of "giving and gaining" that make up the fabric of volunteering — particularly student volunteering. Since she has greatly influenced some of the students who come into contact with her, I have chosen to let Andrea's letter speak for itself:

Before I came to college volunteering was something "other people" did. "Other people" shop at Lord and Taylor; "other people" talk to their guidance counselors; "other people" do lots of things that never seem like real things that I might do. I tried to become a hospital candy-striper once but was either too young or couldn't get there at the right times . . . . It is not clear why, but I felt out of place . . .

At Brandeis University I read to a blind student for a year. That was not really volunteering because the Massachusetts Commission for the Blind paid me. The volunteers were women who came and told Ronni to clean her room. I knew why I was reading — I like Ronni and besides I was getting paid. If these other women were reading just out of the goodness of their hearts, why did they have to tell Ronni to clean her room? That was when I first started thinking about the motives for doing volunteer work.

It seems to me that it is not bad to have ulterior motives for doing good things as long as you understand yourself. If I get a charge out of building my ego by reading to the blind, it is better to do that than to build my ego by robbing banks. I can think of lots of great ulterior motives for reading to the blind. I have made friends and built myself a fair speaking and reading voice with the practice, besides reading lots of interesting stuff. So I feel good about myself. Hopefully so do the people I read to.

When, during my sophomore year, the psychology professor asked me to take over his math tutee, I was flattered and jumped at the chance of doing real *volunteer* work. *(Now I am embarrassed by my suburban radical glee at getting an opportunity of helping* real *people in a* real *ghetto.) Gradually I developed effective techniques of teaching him the math he asked to learn. It went well.*

Then I left Brandeis, worked full time, and transferred to the University of Massachusetts in Boston. During my first semester there I went right back to tutoring at the Upward Bound project. Unfortunately, the students were about as eager to meet with a math tutor as they had been to take math in the first place. I don't think it was any reflection on me particularly that they often "forgot" their appointments. Upward Bound volunteering was rather unproductive, and so a friend and I became school volunteers and taught folk dancing once a week at an elementary school in Brighton. Besides being great fun, that volunteer experience had long-range benefits for both of us. My friend received a tentative "be sure to come by when you graduate" job offer. The school volunteer office asked our psychology teacher for our return the following year. Our professor had never received such a letter about any of her students before and has since written me a glowing letter of recommendation which has helped me no end in my job hunting.

Meanwhile the months of sitting in that Upward Bound office waiting for forgetful tutees to show up were beginning to impress the director of the program that I was, if nothing else, a faithful volunteer. He hired me for the summer as a tutor counselor in mathematics.

That fall, because of my previous volunteer experience, I got a part-time job with a Youth Activities Commission project training volunteer reading tutors. I found out then that I myself am much happier when I can do the actual tutoring than when I have to manage, train, and supervise other tutors. I was learning about my strengths and weaknesses, and I was being paid to do what I wanted to do.

After that things just rolled along. One job led to the next, another summer at an Upward Bound project in upstate New York, a tutoring job in South Boston. In that way volunteering has led me to great paying jobs, has taught me about myself, and has been a very important part of my education. In retrospect, I feel that rather than having given my time and energy to other people as a volunteer, they gave a great deal to me . . . .

At the University of Massachusetts Placement Office I was soon promoted to part-time and summer-placement officer. Students come in demanding paid jobs relevant to their majors. They claim they are too busy to volunteer and besides, they say, they need the money. I explain as best I can that these jobs are difficult to come by and that I rarely hear of such openings. But I can't help thinking that an agency would do well to give job preference to someone who had shown some tangible interest and gained some experience through previous volunteer work. I can give students and others a lot of valid reasons why I think it pays to take the time to become a volunteer. At the risk of sounding like an evangelist, here are some of them:

—Volunteering might lead to a part-time job. (It did for me.)
—Volunteering will introduce the volunteer to people and agencies who might some day open the door to a full-time job.
—Volunteering usually means good recommendations for employment or graduate school.
—Volunteering might mean academic credit. Senior honors or directed study is always more flexible than they told you it would be if you approach the department with a good project already in progress.
—Volunteering helps you make decisions about what you want to do and about what you might be good at doing. (It is very hard to be a graduating social science major who only knows that he wants to "work with people.")
—Volunteering gives meaning to course work and helps stave off that

unsettling "moratorium on life" feeling.
— Volunteering might result in learning something.

  . . . The students know how I feel, and more and more of them come to my office asking for volunteer placements. I have pleaded with the administration to establish a student volunteer service center and have let them know that I see a large number of students interested in volunteering who have no idea how to find a suitable placement for themselves. Finally, I wrote a proposal for a Student Volunteer Center and submitted it to the University Funding Office. I know that it is under serious consideration but depends, like so much else, on whether the already severely taxed budget can be stretched yet a little further.

9

The Working Woman
(and the Working Man)

About ten years ago an article in *Boston Magazine*, which devoted an entire issue to the working woman, described her as being between two worlds. "Stepping from adolescence toward womanhood, experiencing a wonderfully new weird world . . . of happiness and disappointment, ambition and boredom, confidence and uneasiness, loneliness and love, and above all breaking the pattern of over twenty years of rigid routine: a time to taste delicious new freedoms, and, in turn, to face new responsibilities."

Although entering the working world after graduation still brings with it some of that excitement and sense of adventure, I would say that for the educated woman it no longer represents an "in-between world," a way station between school and marriage. The joy and despair resulting from intense personal relationships are experienced at an ever earlier age; teenagers travel here, there, and everywhere; excitement enters their lives often prematurely, wears off fast, and needs to be replaced with novel experiences. By the time the working woman settles down she may well have run the gamut of exciting experiences, including the drug scene, and may in fact feel slightly jaded.

To me, perhaps the most telling phrase in the magazine
description of the working woman is "to face new responsibilities." To be sure, there are responsibilities inherent in
any new position, but they become routine rather quickly,
and frequently it turns out to be the lack of challenge from the
actual job that makes the young woman — or man, for that
matter — search elsewhere for involvement and commitment.

Work Routine Relieved Through Alternate Community Service

When Frances was hired by one of the home
offices of a large insurance company, she found herself at a
desk among a sea of identical desks in a large, well-lit room,
with telephones ringing and typewriters banging away all
around her. Frances has training and likes to work with figures
and statistics; yet she found herself impatiently watching the
clock, longing for a coffee break, a smoke, or lunch. Five o'clock
seemed to roll around painfully slowly. When she learned that
a few of her colleagues were working one or two days a week
in the city's public schools, she decided that instead of quitting
her job, she would ask for time off during the day to work as a
school volunteer twice a week, offering to make up the lost
hours in overtime. The company granted her request and six
months later gave her released time without requiring any
overtime from her. An analysis of Frances' performance
showed that she had been putting forth more and better work
on her limited schedule than she had on the full five-day 9-5
regime.

Encouraged by her boss's enthusiasm and cooperation, she
began to interest other employees in volunteer work either in
the city or in their own communities. When the company
suggested organizing a forum on community work at the in-
house cafeteria during the lunch hour, Frances was a rich
source of information on the kinds of exciting things

volunteers could do and learn at various schools around the city. She herself had chosen to team up with another school volunteer to work with a group of "special" students with severe hearing defects who were thrilled by the tactile and visual experience which a course in Japanese flower arranging provided for them.

Employees Take the Initiative

Meanwhile, at another big insurance company, women *and* men on the company's payroll became interested in community service. Among the reasons given was a genuine concern for the people and problems of the adjacent neighborhood, just a few blocks away from the company's office tower. After consultation with city volunteer placement offices, a few members of the personnel department staff, together with fellow employees, petitioned management to sponsor an employee organization which would develop and operate a clearinghouse for those employees both active and retired, who were anxious to volunteer for community service. Their proposal — which could easily serve as a model for business and industry — brought approval and implementation; the Volunteer-Action Clearinghouse was created.

Proposal:

> That the company sponsor an employee organization that will develop and operate a clearinghouse for their active and retired employees who wish to volunteer their free time in community service.

Objective:

> Volunteer-Action Clearinghouse will perform the function of matching the skills and interests of these volunteers with the needs of appropriate community-service organizations. The clearinghouse will encourage, recruit, interview, and place volunteer employees in various community-service agencies and maintain a list of specific needs of these agencies.

Implementation:

   1. Receive approval of proposal from personnel and budget-control committee.
   2. Establish a location within the home office to be designated the Volunteer-Action Clearinghouse.
   3. Staff the clearinghouse with volunteer interviewers during lunch hours.
   4. Publicize the clearinghouse and its goals through the news weekly, bulletins, and other means.
   5. Distribute a questionnaire seeking employee-volunteer interests.

Costs:

   1. Office space, supplies, and furniture
   2. Telephone
   3. Publicity

Benefits:

   1. Reaffirm the company's commitment to assist the community via our most valuable resource — people.
   2. Provide an inexpensive fringe benefit for employees and retirees who need help to find volunteer activities.

The following are some excerpts from an article in the company's weekly:

SOMEONE NEEDS YOU . . . . You. Not your money. This isn't another request for a dollar-and-cents contribution. We're inviting you to contribute a little bit of yourself, to give a few hours a week spent caring about somebody else, to help someone who needs you: a youngster with nobody to turn to, an oldster longing for companionship, a human being trying to find a place in society. People, much like you, but different because they need something only you can give — time.

The word is "Volunteer." The Volunteer-Action Clearinghouse *makes it easy for you to get started.*

Formed by a group of employees, VAC will put you in contact with a variety of community agencies, institutions, and projects that need your help.

Initially, several of the employees who developed VAC will provide their interviewing skills to help fellow employees link their interests with community needs.

Other members will check out agencies requesting volunteers to make certain they offer you the best opportunity for meaningful community participation.

A followup procedure will be established to assure that both volunteers and agencies served by VAC are fully satisfied.

VAC's office is open to all interested employees. If you are ready to help someone, complete the questionnaire and set up an appointment. Interview hours are from 11:30 to 2:00 every Tuesday and Thursday.

Some of the typical volunteer opportunities which company employees chose included working at hospitals, halfway houses, schools for the handicapped and the disadvantaged, alcoholism treatment centers, and a neighborhood center for Spanish-speaking people.

The success of the employees' volunteer program is in part responsible for the company's extension of their four-day work week experiment to many more employees.

Released Time

Banks, manufacturing firms, and utility companies are also taking tentative steps in the direction of community involvement for their employees and are experimenting, very cautiously at first, with company released time. Companies are beginning to exchange ideas, compare their experiences, and help each other with solutions to common problems in the area of community involvement. Up for discussion are such questions as: How do you choose men and women eligible for released time? What of the boss who finds it irritating when his or her secretary is gone for the afternoon recording for the blind and is not available for a revision or a rush job that day?

The following is taken from an article on volunteering from a company publication:

> *Volunteering in any form is one of man's finer attributes. Volunteers are, by definition, people seeking greater dimensions in their lives. Technology has enabled most of us to fulfill basic security needs with little effort; but in a peculiar twist of irony, this factor responsible for easier survival may be blurring the avenues to fulfillment of our more complex needs.*
>
> *A return to the community, the community of working with others, joining in common causes. Getting out of ourselves, working with others, we begin to find ourselves again.*

Women with Irregular Work Schedules

While it is more usual for the working woman to volunteer on a regular weekly basis throughout the year, I have learned about several interesting variations on this theme.

We have been consulted by a number of airline stewardesses at our placement agency. These women are in search of suitable volunteer opportunities, but their schedules vary so much that regular once-or-twice-a-week assignments at the same locale and at the same time are quite unrealistic. Louise S. Davidson, director of volunteer services at Bellevue Hospital Center in New York, used her imagination and decided to link airline stewardesses wth the home care department of her hospital. Her experience showed that "the chronically ill or physically handicapped are often out of touch with family and friends . . . i.e., socially isolated." She found that airline stewardesses by virtue of their training and sensitivity are especially suited for patient-contact work. And, as one might guess, she also found them "often lonely, many far from home, in a strange city, knowing few people." She matched twenty carefully chosen housebound patients with ten volunteers, and so started a "friendship-by-telephone" service.

The following is from *Volunteer Action News,* August 1972:

>   *During training, the Director of Home Care
> described the living conditions and interests of the chosen patients.
> Discussions focused on how to open and close a telephone
> conversation with a stranger. Role-playing put the volunteers on the
> receiving end of the calls to help them understand what kinds of
> attitudes and conversation would be most welcome and helpful.*
>
>   *The volunteers helped assign themselves to two patients each. For
> example, one patient was a former foreign correspondent. An airline
> volunteer who had traveled extensively felt they might have common
> interests and experiences to talk about.*
>
>   *The volunteers were told to call Home Care immediately with any
> problems mentioned by patients that required quick action. Forms, due
> in the Volunteer Department at the end of the month, were provided
> for information about each call — date, length of conversation,
> general comments.*
>
>   *Patients and volunteers discuss a wide variety of subjects in these
> telephone visits, including some problems the patients consider too
> insignificant to mention to a doctor, nurse or social worker.*
>
>   *For example, a patient tells a volunteer that she really doesn't
> understand what the doctor tells her. The volunteer relays this to the
> patient's Home Care nurse and the doctor's instructions are given
> more carefully.*
>
>   *Mrs. S., also a Home Care patient, lost her husband not long ago.
> She was lonely and frightened to be living by herself. With the help of
> her social worker and Home Care nurse, Mrs. S. has become a Person-
> to-Person volunteer calling other home-bound patients.*

The need and the volunteer power exist in other cities, too.
What a great project for a "take-charge person" to develop;
perhaps the Visiting Nurses could provide the professional
link.

Taking the Summer Off for Volunteering

Smoki, who has been cited as an outstand-
ing professional woman, is also considered a prime mover

and shaker of some dozen volunteer efforts. She cares greatly about people and causes and has enormous energy. What is so special about Smoki is the fact that each year she takes the entire summer off from her regular job — that of a graphic artist. She is the creator of a "crafts-mobile" unit which she fills with art supplies of all kinds collected throughout the year: crayons, paper, cardboard, scraps of fabric, recycled containers, old spools, string, etc. Then she staffs the vans with enthusiastic young volunteers, her own two children among them. It is a strenuous job and not much of a vacation;

sometimes even her volunteers need recycling! During the long hot summers, the mini-buses fan out to different parts of the city, and each day volunteers set up shop in housing projects, playgrounds, and supermarket parking lots. The neighborhood children come swarming: the Pied Piper of Hamlin could do no better.

Volunteering Between Paid Jobs

Highly skilled and successful personnel sometimes find themselves out in the street unexpectedly. After Edith's firm was bought by another publishing house, her department was phased out. Edith, a senior editor, was out of work.

She began searching for an equivalent position. After several discouraging weeks, Edith found that the only jobs available were for unskilled labor or secretarial help. She toyed with the idea of taking a dishwasher's job, but eventually passed it up; something inside her rebelled against this total waste of her real talents and expertise.

Finally she realized that she would have to apply for unemployment insurance, something she did not undertake lightly—it went against the grain. Her application approved, she qualified for 39 weeks of unemployment benefits.

Edith continued to search for a suitable opening, sending out resumes and going to interviews. But she knew that the search would not give her enough to do every day.

Not wishing to become despondent and utterly ineffective, she looked for a voluntary position to maintain her spirits and to keep an eye open for possible leads to paid employment. She chose to work with a group giving voluntary technical assistance around the world. Her fluency in Italian enabled her to help draft proposals for saving art treasures damaged by water in Venice. After translating primary source material gathered by Italian experts, she then used her skill as an experienced editor to help draft succinct and explicit funding proposals. Edith was determined not to feel useless while waiting for her next salaried position. She has since become a college lecturer in French literature who commutes out of state.

Sabbaticals for Volunteering

The Xerox Corporation, long considered a company with a social conscience, has instituted an experimental Social Service Leave program. Twenty men and women, chosen from nearly 2,000 applicants, take leaves from their regular jobs to concentrate on Social Welfare projects of their own choosing. Leaves up to one year come complete with full pay and benefits. When they return, these volunteers are guaranteed the same positions they left or similar ones.

This is an attempt to "give formal status to what other companies are doing informally." Significantly, these volunteers represent a cross section of the entire company — men and women from more than ten states, from distributors to corporate vice presidents, ranging in age from 26 to 60.

Lisa is the recipient of one such sabbatical. Formerly a schoolteacher, she has been with Xerox for seven years in the educational publications department. For her "volunteer job," she will work with the elderly, something she already does in her spare time; Xerox helped her to secure a position with a state department of the elderly.

Lisa has long wanted to have the chance to work full-time in this way, and her year off will provide it:

> When I did volunteer work before, I always felt I wasn't doing enough. Sure, I would spend time helping others, but I would spend 40 hours a week working for myself. Now I will be able to devote all my time and energies to something I really care about . . . I know that some people would not take part in this program, because they are afraid to miss a chance for promotion. Anyone who looks at it in that way need not apply . . .

Volunteering a Professional Skill

There are many professional men and women who enjoy successful careers and also do volunteer work related to their regular jobs. They feel not only that volunteering is personally enriching, but that, as professionals, they can contribute their special know-how to groups in need.

In the old, established, well-paid professions, particularly in law and medicine, there is a long-standing tradition of volunteer service. Some doctors have always given free service in clinics and on hospital wards. Lawyers abound among the trustees and unpaid officers of voluntary agencies of all kinds, and for generations many of them have represented poor clients for free—as volunteers.

Here, too, the scope of volunteer service is changing—changing in magnitude and in kind. Literally hundreds of young lawyers in many big cities now supplement the government-supported public defenders in representing criminal defendants, particularly in the lowest courts. In their "free" time, young doctors—and the not so young—staff mobile medical units and community clinics that render medical services to the lost and disenchanted amoung our people, who for one reason or another can no longer be reached by established institutions. Architects and planners act as volunteer advisors to neighborhood groups. They may help these groups develop plans that can be offered as alternatives to objectionable changes about to be imposed on them. And the same lawyers who in the past might have given their volunteer time to a large hospital or museum, might now volunteer to represent that neighborhood in court battles and before the legislature to get the neighborhood plan, rather than the imposed one, adopted.

But volunteering by full-time professionals is by no means confined to lawyers and doctors and architects or planners.

Christine is a young filmmaker who runs her own business. Her combined training in urban affairs and documentary-film work makes her a natural for a very particular kind of community service. She has managed to inspire some troubled teenagers by leading an experimental film workshop. While they usually have to beg or borrow film and equipment, these youths are so excited about being able to express themselves through film that Christine says, "I wouldn't miss it for the world . . . I have even let some regular commissions slip by when they might have interfered with what we are trying to do in the workshop."

Joan, another young professional woman, is a full-time field program advisor for the Girl Scouts, an organization which is consciously trying to update its traditional activities. Through a coordinated regional policy of innovative community relations programs, she and others like her hope to eliminate the old stereotypes and create a new image for the Girl Scout movement.

To show her true commitment to social change, Joan also volunteers as a nighttime counselor at a neighborhood multiservice center in addition to her normal duties with the Scouts. At first she worked Sunday nights from 7 p.m. to 7 a.m., followed by a full workweek and two nights of school. When she found this schedule too exhausting, she switched to a Wednesday night assignment at the service center and carried a smaller course load.

At the service center, Joan works under the supervision of a social worker and psychiatrist. Some of her work is crisis-oriented, but she has many continuing clients and generally finds those relationships the most satisfying. She has commented that:

> There is very little absenteeism among our regular volunteers, and we feel a real team spirit and great sense of commitment. Personally, I find that my volunteer experience adds to a better understanding of my work with the Scouts . . . and provides a needed service here in the community.

Volunteering and Sports

Sports pros are no exception. Among many available examples, I like that of a tennis club—of all things—established in the heart of a big city to give inner-city kids the chance to play tennis and to be coached to achieve tournament-quality standards, and possibly to become pros themselves. I like this example because here an entirely new program was established out of the imagination, enthusiasm, and hard work of many different kinds of volunteers. An expert on tennis court construction volunteered his advice and, when the facilities were there, gave the special teaching aids he had designed for his own tennis camp in the country. He also brought his coaches to the city to train the instructors for the new club. A well-known sportscaster volunteered to help get the idea off the ground and to raise needed money. Once the idea had caught on, tennis enthusiasts in large numbers chipped in with volunteer assistance. Even Arthur Ashe came to run a tennis clinic. The sparkplug of the entire operation was a determined black tennis buff, a government employee, who—disappointed with the city's recreational facilities and efforts to improve them—gave hours, days, weeks, and months of his own time to realize his dream of providing tennis courts and instruction for the youngsters in his neighborhood. And he succeeded beyond all expectation!

In short, the ferment of new volunteer opportunities permeates all working life for fully employed women and men, from secretaries to filmmakers to social workers and sports pros. It has also not passed by the older, established professions; there, a deeply rooted tradition of volunteering, which in the past has been heavily Establishment-oriented, is expanding into new fields and interests. The causes of the poor, the minorities, women, and environmentalists are only a few among those offering challenge and satisfaction to the volunteering professional woman and man.

10

The Mother of Young Children

Would it be facetious to assert that certain mothers are volunteer workers by nature? Nobody tells them to toil from morning till night; nobody pays them. Does anybody appreciate the work they do? One often wonders.

Yet it is usual for many mothers to take on volunteer tasks outside the home, often in connection with the activities of their children or extended family. They work in day-care centers, in cooperative nursery schools. They become den and scout mothers; they join the PTA and lobby the local school committee; they organize benefits and fairs. They work as volunteers for a myriad of fund drives, they help at the Red Cross blood bank, and they drive the elderly, the handicapped, or visitors from abroad, often on short notice. They work in their children's schools and libraries assisting the paid staff. They sit on the boards of voluntary associations of all kinds from Visiting Nurses to Fair Housing committees. They are members of the League of Women Voters or, in the last few years, of NOW. Political candidates depend on their organizational talents, particularly at election time. Hospital auxiliaries could not function without them. Churches, synagogues, museums — all vie for their help.

Is there a limit to the number of mothers who are prepared to give of themselves, of their special talents, all without pay,

all for the sake of a cause they believe in or simply because a job needs to be done and there is nobody else to do it?

I find there is an unlimited supply of such women of good will. In fact, it is my conviction that some of the most willing and efficient young women, the ones most apt to be called upon, must learn early to say no to the never-ending requests for volunteer help. They must determine what they consider important and how they wish to expend their energies (what has meaning for *them*), make their choice, and stick to it. Those who do not learn this difficult lesson of the polite but firm no are the ones who become bitter and vocal about volunteer work and sooner or later turn against it completely. How often have I heard the refrain, usually from the mother of somewhat older children, "I am fed up with being a volunteer; I want a *real* job now. I want a job that pays." Given her previous experience, this woman's about-face is almost inevitable; and society pays a high price for making such indiscriminate demands on young mothers. Granted, there are other compelling reasons for turning one's back on volunteer work.

Mothers, especially of young children, are at home a good

part of the day and can easily be reached there. It is natural to call on the members of this captive group for help of all kinds. Of course, there are things which a mother can do while at home, but these activities do little to alleviate her often-present sense of isolation from stimulating adult company. Often the volunteer obligations just add more strain. Try making a few telephone calls with toddlers underfoot! Yet this is one of the pet favors that is asked of housebound mothers. Mailings are another perennial volunteer chore for mothers at home.

Enabling Young Mothers to Do Volunteer Work Away From Home

Helena Z. Lopata confirms in her thoughtful study *Occupation Housewife** that women with young children — that is, with more than one offspring, the youngest of whom is less than nine years old — feel most isolated and need to increase their contact with people. A young mother may mind the absence of a work rhythm she had become used to before her first child was born. She may jump at the chance to get out of the house, only to find scheduling extremely difficult. In order for her to volunteer outside the home, adequate baby-sitting arrangements will have to be available. Some real breakthroughs are occurring to enable mothers of small children to volunteer during the day without having to arrange for baby sitters.**

The Museum of Science is leading the way in Boston by providing child-care facilities at the museum while mothers volunteer. So far, these facilities are available only at very limited times. The volunteers themselves suggested that they

---

*Helena Z. Lopata, *Occupation Housewife* (Fairlawn, N.J.: Oxford University Press, 1971), p. 34.

**Tax deductibility of baby-sitting expenses for working mothers has not fared well recently. For further discussion, see Part One, Chapter 6, "The Idea of the Volunteer Professional," pp. 34-43. .

bring their children with them rather than pay hard-to-find baby sitters at home, and to take turns being in charge of the nursery every fourth or fifth week. With the help of the experienced and flexible volunteer director at the museum, the volunteer staff thought through and worked out medical and liability problems. The experiment at the Museum of Science has already inspired others in Boston and vicinity. The New England Aquarium may soon follow suit, and the Cambridge Center for Adult Education is considering a similar arrangement.

It is a big commitment for an institution to offer child-care service for the purpose of attracting or holding a group of volunteers who would otherwise not be able to serve. For the hospital, museum, or school, with suitable space often at a

premium, this entails a good deal of both financial and legal
responsibility. This arrangement cannot be entered into
lightly, and the returns must warrant the effort. For the
mother of small children, such a cooperative child-care
project affords the chance to get out of the house, meet others,
and contribute to the community. For the children it is a gay
morning or afternoon of playing with different toys and
learning to share with others. It may even be a way of easing a
child into a full-time day-care center. Also, such cooperative
set-ups might help eliminate the guilt felt by many young
mothers when they decide to "abandon" their offspring to
"strangers" all day, every day — and particularly so when it
is "only" a personal interest or a volunteer job they wish to
pursue.

I believe that the kind of experiment conducted at the
Museum of Science bears watching, needs strong support in
its initial stages, and should encourage other institutions to
work out their own adaptations of the model. These child-
care arrangements serve the needs of the mothers, the young
children, and those in need of volunteer help. Institutions will
do themselves a huge favor if they tackle the task with
boldness and imagination.

Other Child-Care Arrangements

Some women have formed play groups on
their own and rotate taking care of each other's children at
their respective homes. One group of mothers I know is
including the preschool daughter of a woman separated from
her husband while she works to supplement the child support
she receives. Neighbors helping neighbors, perhaps, but it *is*
an effective kind of volunteer effort and most supportive of
the mother who cannot take her turn at supervising the
playgroup.

I have also learned of several baby-sitting pools in suburbs
near major cities which have been formed with the express

purpose of freeing mothers for volunteer service away from home on a regular weekly basis. An elaborate point system keeps track of the number of hours contributed by the members, and service points can be collected during day or evening hours. Husbands, too, wishing to help their wives gain time off from domestic duties for the volunteer work of their choice, may chalk up points for them.

There are always special problems for mothers trying to balance domestic duties and work away from home. Everyone knows that young children do become sick quite often and unexpectedly, and when they must stay home, so must Mother! Yet, even though cooperative playgroups, baby-sitting pools, or day-care centers cannot provide complete answers, it seems to me that a little ingenuity, plenty of good will, and a certain amount of determination can go a long way to enable greater numbers of mothers of young children to participate in voluntary service outside the home — a choice which seemed quite impractical until now.

Sweden is a country from which we might profitably borrow some good techniques which can, much like tempting French cookbook recipes, be adapted for use in this country. Sweden, with its progressive political and social structure, is far ahead in its development of equal opportunities for both men and women.* We can learn much and we need new ideas for freeing mothers for alternate work, both paid and unpaid.

Profile of Two Friends

Bonny and Mameve are both young married women. Each has two children under four; both are attractive, intelligent, and vivacious. When I visited with them one wintry morning — the first day of nursery school vacation — they were both wearing pants and cotton velour and jersey tops, respectively. Both their husbands practice law.

*See "The Emancipation of Man," by Olof Palme, Prime Minister of Sweden, in *The Journal of Social Issues*, Vol. 28, No. 2, 1972.

That is where the outward similarity ends, I think. One woman is Catholic, the other Jewish; one comes from Maryland, the other grew up in Maine. One majored in English and has never held a paying job; the other has a master's degree in Spanish studies and has taught at both a high school and a junior college. They also differ in some of their opinions about volunteer work.

What is unusual about them is that their two families bought a one-family house together and converted it so that each family now has a separate, self-contained apartment. They have retained the nuclear family concept of privacy in most respects but share the care of each other's children during the daytime whenever convenient. Mameve has finished fixing up her apartment, which is full of plants and paintings; while Bonny is working feverishly at remodeling her part of the house, which is still in a topsy-turvy state.

They have worked out an interesting cooking arrangement among themselves and another neighbor. A unique twice-a-week cooperative meal plan allows each woman one afternoon off per week, yet does not result in communal dining, something which all three families wish to avoid.

Thus Bonny and Mameve have regular free time to do with as they please, a luxury not often available to mothers of young children.

I asked them about their volunteer experience prior to marriage and whether they are considering volunteer work now or in the future. Here is what they have to say:

Bonny and Mameve: Because of our living situation, we do not suffer from the usual symptoms of housebound young mothers. We are not physically isolated, we do have close neighbors, and friends are always in and out; what's more, stores and restaurants are a block away. We can exchange baby-sitting, and our cooperative cooking arrangement gives us extra freedom.

It seems to us that the need to "get out" is often confused with the need for personal gratification. In all honesty we resent the demands made on us by what we think of as "volunteer work" — fundraising, telephoning, and chores related to our children's school. We both already have our hands full and never have enough time. Sure we would like to do something useful for others, and find it hard to say no, but we don't like to be manipulated. Both of us have been turned off by previous unsuccessful volunteer work, and for once we want to do something that is a treat, not a treatment.

Mameve: I am particularly skeptical about being a volunteer. I once tried to work with a disorganized and uninterested bunch of drama students. I have never had a regular paying job, and I would like to prove to myself that I can be financially independent. Yet I am the first to concede that our society is too money-oriented and that success should not be measured in dollars and cents alone. If just the right opportunity came along, I might feel differently about working as a volunteer. I don't feel a sense of shame or guilt which would make me go in search of just the perfect opening. I guess in the end it is really a question of temperament.

Bonny: In many ways my reaction is similar. When I was in high school I worked with senile patients in a home. I don't know what made me do it. I dreaded every Tuesday when I had to report for work. Yet at the same time I felt terrible about my lack of sympathy for the old men and women cooped up in their rooms. I wish someone had told me that this kind of volunteer work is very difficult for most people, and that I was perhaps expecting too much of myself.

I have looked into the possibility of putting my knowledge of Spanish to some use. I read about a neighborhood clinic that needs an interpreter. But since I'm thinking going to law school, I would prefer to volunteer in a legal-aid office with Spanish- and Portuguese-speaking clients.

Bonny and Mameve: When you come right down to it, we both do some volunteer work we enjoy immensely: we act as host families for foreign students. We always have so much fun with them that we never consider it "volunteering" ...

Profile of Two Teachers

Ruth is thirty-five years old, the mother of two girls (four and six), her husband is a professional man, and she is lucky enough to have a remarkably able young mother's helper. She herself is a college graduate and holds a Master of Arts in Teaching. With short interruptions she has taught English in high school and thoroughly enjoys teaching. It seems she has always done some volunteer work, often taking a leadership role, but lately — with her part-time teaching job eliminated — she has become heavily involved in politics at the grass-roots level. Her volunteer work consumed most of her days and many evenings. She definitely overextended herself and feels that she may in part have used the excessive volunteer involvement (with some success) to fend off depression. Now teaching again, she has cut down on her extracurricular activities and has sworn never to work so hard again without being paid; she says she prefers to compete in the marketplace. A stint as a volunteer teacher working alongside paid staff was a disappointment and an exercise in frustration for her. Her colleagues did not consider her an equal even though her professional training was on a par with theirs, and she was definitely not accepted as a member of the faculty. For her and others like her, volunteering has *not* offered a workable alternative.

Karen is just thirty years old and the mother of a four-month-old baby. She became interested in teaching small children as a volunteer while in college, was a volunteer teacher in Mississippi one summer, and taught in Africa for one year following graduation. After a year at Bank Street College in New York City she became a public schoolteacher at P.S. 113 in the city and prior to her marriage taught for a year at the Walden School.

She and her teacher husband returned to New England, and Karen worked at a community school in Dorchester until her baby was born. When the school's funds ran out, she agreed to return as a consultant on a volunteer basis one day a week. She started when her baby was a month old and takes him with her. She consults with teachers on classroom problems (children, curriculum, etc.) and thoroughly enjoys it. If money should become available, she would accept a salary, but is content to work as a volunteer. She has a similar arrangement in one of the suburbs for one other day where funds have just been allocated. Karen has run teachers' workshops for alternative schools also on a volunteer basis.

At this stage in her life she is very happy with the arrangement. She would not bring her baby to a day-care center and has at present no one to leave him with, although her mother will and often does take him for the day. As long as it remains possible Karen prefers to have her baby with her. Karen's husband gives her full support and helps share housework and child care. She loves teaching and for the time being it allows her all the outside stimulation she needs and enables her to stay in touch with what is happening in her field. The mixture of volunteer and professional engagements suits Karen to perfection.

A Young Mother and a Professional

In her statement, Joan B. Honig discusses what volunteering means to her at this particular stage and gives some concrete suggestions on how to integrate the professional person more successfully into volunteer organizations.

"Volunteer work plays a very important role in my life at this particular time.

"I am thirty years old, a lawyer, and the wife of a corporate lawyer. I am a mother of three small children. Currently I view my primary responsibility as seeing that my children develop into stable, happy individuals. My husband and I have come to the conclusion that, since his job demands that he be away from home for extended periods, I should remain at home with the children.

"Since I do not want to be cut off from the world of action and adult ideas during this decade of child rearing, I have looked to volunteering to bridge this period for me. In this context, I utilize volunteer work in three ways: as a method of keeping myself intellectually acute, as a method of training myself for future employment, and as an opportunity to pursue areas of interest to the extent and at the pace I find comfortable.

"I view part-time volunteerism as an exciting learning experience.

"My own volunteer work is divided into two areas — legal and nonlegal. As an unpaid attorney I have functioned in a variety of ways. I have done legal research in civil liberties, drafting and revison of statutes and bylaws, and advising and representing clients in fields like student rights.

"As a lay volunteer I have also functioned in a variety of capacities: as a member of a board of directors in several groups, as a politician, as an officer of a group, as chairman of a large and effective committee, as a member of a prestigious advisory board, and as a contributing member of a League of Women Voters study group.

"Experts in many areas freely grant me their time and consideration, simply because of my various volunteer affiliations. Conferences, meetings, and dialogues with interesting strangers wait for me constantly. I can be as deeply or as marginally committed as I choose . . . and without the pressures and restraints of employment which would, however subtly, filter down to my children. Because I work for no one but myself, I have the freedom to experiment with my interests and to create new areas of exploration. I have learned many concrete skills. Additionally, it is easier to rapidly accumulate a good deal of status and responsibility as a lay volunteer than as a professional and this does tremendous things for my ego.

"I do not view volunteer work as remedial as much as preventive. I plan to avoid the feeling of ineptitude that frequently is the companion of suburban woman when she contemplates return, after years of exile, to the urban scene.

"Granted that volunteerism is to me an educational and training experience that fulfills me without interfering with what I view to be my principal function at this time — this arrangement has certain annoying drawbacks inherent in the structure of volunteerism itself.

"Volunteer organizations typically have the problems of weak leadership, lack of overall direction and purpose, and a scarcity of people who are actually involved and working, as well as many other shortcomings. Perhaps professional volunteering can suggest some solutions:

"1. Members in almost any group could profitably be offered a choice of finite pieces of work, perhaps to be done individually rather than in committee.

"2. More respect should be had for members' time. Meetings should have stated beginnings and endings. The busy individual who might be able to make a meaningful contribution to an organization is frequently annoyed by the trivial discussion that robs the group of valuable work time.

"3. Furthermore, volunteer organizations should consider in certain circumstances providing their members with assigned secretarial help and if necessary pay for it out of the treasury. Even in fund-raising organizations the cost might well be justified by the increased efficiency and contribution of the members.

"4. In volunteer groups where people are unwilling to take on the larger and more time-consuming projects, for free, perhaps there should be the possibility of hiring a person in the group to act as a paid consultant on a particular project.

"5. Even more important than financial recognition is the need for *formal recognition* of the scope of the volunteer's achievement in the group. Perhaps a certificate, routinely given. In education there are credit hours, and in the work force there are wages, but there is no standard unit of measure of volunteer work. While the simple number of hours worked might do for the Red Cross or the hospitals, a more sophisticated method is necessary in the other types of groups.

"Notwithstanding these problems, I strongly advocate my solution: to pace oneself and combine volunteer activities with child rearing."

11

The Returnee to Work

Who is she? She is likely to be in her thirties or forties, and has spent the last ten to twenty years primarily occupied with family obligations. She realizes these obligations are decreasing and no longer require so much of her time and energy.

Usually the "empty nest syndrome" occurs when the children grow up and begin to leave home, particularly when the youngest child is becoming a teenager alarmingly fast. The offspring are likely to let it be known by kind — or not so kind — words, body language, and behavior in general, that they wish to be more independent and want less attention and fussing over. These are healthy signals, but they often make the mother feel superfluous. In some families it may be the mother herself who feels that her turn has come, that she has done her share for the family, and that it is time she thought a little more of herself and her own interests.

Most likely she is influenced by the trend of the times, and it need not be her children who trigger the reaction. It may be women's liberation, her friends' activities, or recognition of the multitude of society's problems which need attention, possibly even *her* attention. Perhaps her husband's expectations may lead a woman to question the time and energy which go into being a "housewife"; she may change her mind about spending most of her time at home.

But no matter what causes the sense of "housewifely overkill," a woman first needs to find another focus for involvement. She will become aware, whether dramatically or only gradually and dimly, through a sense of dissatisfaction, that she is lost and at loose ends, that she must find something "new." "There must be more to life than this" is almost a theme song among this group of women who come for help and advice.

Settling for doing less for the family is likely to prove frustrating and unsatisfactory. These women surely can gain greater contentment by channeling newly freed energies, but, in order to make a shift in their involvement, they must first define what it is they would like to shift to.

How to Take the Next Step

This chapter, then, is about the problems and pitfalls faced by the woman who wishes to return to work and some practical suggestions as to how to deal with them, including a description of tools and techniques which can be helpful in the process. In this chapter I will attempt to show how volunteering can be an extremely positive temporary or permanent solution for the returnee to work.

Years of responsibility for husband, children, and household have matured and changed the prospective returnee principally in the following ways:

1. Almost certainly, she will have increased her competence as manager, organizer, and administrator and her ability to deal with people. Often women are not aware of the giant steps they have made in developing their own management skills.

2. She will probably find her competence reduced in any field in which she had specialized before marriage and children.

3. She has additional interests and different expectations and aspirations.

At the present time the typical "returnee" tends to emerge from years of absorption in her family without clear professional goals.

Dual Commitment

Lifestyles are rapidly changing, and total devotion to a family for a decade or two is becoming rarer. Young women, even with children, are not dropping out of the work force to the same extent that their mothers did before them. If dual commitment to family and outside involvement is maintained, returning to work is greatly facilitated. It is entirely conceivable that among certain groups of women there will be no "return to work" as such but, as the children grow up, only a redistribution of work between home and outside. If this present trend continues, it is quite possible that this chapter will be obsolete and could be left out of a 1980 equivalent of this book.

Even now the highly trained professional such as the woman doctor, lawyer, or city planner is able to chart her path as a returnee far more readily. Many of the typical difficulties under discussion in the following pages do not apply to her. Yet, it may come as a surprise that some of the questions to be answered by the not "highly trained" returnee must be answered by the professional woman as well. Indeed, my experience as a counselor and leader of seminars has taught me that one cannot assume that the trained professional woman will recognize herself clearly as such after years of housewifery.

In a course on "Creative Leisure" at the Cambridge Center for Adult Education, designed specifically for the prospective woman returnee, I found that fourteen out of sixteen participants gave "housewife" as their occupation on the registration cards. One enterprising woman designated herself as "homemaker," another as "philanthropist." On closer scrutiny, this group turned out to include two nurses, three teachers, a musician, a woman with a Ph.D. in French literature, a librarian, a skilled court stenographer fluent in Spanish, and a former department-store buyer. Yet to a woman, not one of them thought of herself as having a profession! (I wonder whether it would make a difference if the application card specified "profession" instead of "occupation.") What is more, almost none of them wished or expected to go back to the field in which she had been trained. One overly involved woman joined the class hoping to find a focus on one or two interests instead of constantly feeling pulled in all directions. By the end of the course, one mother of fairly young children felt less guilty about playing tennis in her free time and found that she was not ready for either a volunteer or paid job. In all likelihood she will first try a volunteer job "for size" when she does decide to return to work. Interestingly, two years later registration ran very much along the same lines, except for the greater number of younger women who enrolled, anxious to prepare early for the time of "return to work."

These women, consciously or subconsciously, were quite realistic in their assessments. They have added to their competence in many fields, they have lost expertise in others, and they have grown into maturer human beings with a shift in their interests. They had become principally and foremost "housewives."

Erma Bombeck in one of her amusing newspaper columns — "Can there be a better word for Housewife?"—hits the nail on the head when she says she "likes the idea that the housewife's profession is indescribable in three lines or twenty. It means we lead such a varied existence and touch so many areas, it leaves men and women who write the dictionaries at a loss for words." Think of the many components that go into making up the whole housewife: personality, education, training, talents, skills, and, last but not least, mountains of common sense.

Naturally women differ widely in the way they weave their particular cloth of housewifery, using many different strands of yarn due to varying ability, background, education, and experience. What emerges then is a far richer texture of skills than is normally associated with a "mere" housewife.

In that sense, the members of the seminar now had truly become "housewives" and no longer considered themselves "nurse," "librarian," etc. If they had any professional training before marriage, they probably lost touch and did not stay abreast of new developments in their fields during the intervening years. And the woman returnee at re-entry, even with special training and experience, will find novel concepts and ideas, new theories and techniques, no matter what her area of expertise.

Not only will the woman find the working world around her considerably changed, she will also discover that some of her skills have grown rusty, that things are no longer done the way she used to do them. Even in the clerical and managerial category, automatic typewriters, dictaphones, Xerox machines, and computers have revolutionized office procedures.

Most significantly, the potential returnee is ten to fifteen years older now, has made new friends, and has meanwhile developed interests which have opened up new horizons.

Is she sure her profession will still satisfy her? And if so, how can she best use her skills now? Can she pick up where she left off if she wants to? Or could she use her skills in other imaginative ways more in line with the kind of person she has become?

When Betty calls herself a "housewife" rather than a commercial artist on the application form, she may be saying that her interests have changed. After an interval of twelve years, Betty had in fact gone back to school to get a master's degree in painting. She found that she dreaded facing a blank canvas in the studio every day. Although she had realized that she did not want to be a freelance artist again, she discovered a real need to be with and work with people. She also found that she had become far more service-oriented. Having gone through a divorce herself she became intensely interested in the problems of newly divorced women and volunteered to organize a group of such women for self-help and self-support. She eventually went to work in continuing education for women, and painting has become an enjoyable avocation.

Self-Analysis

Aware that her family's demands on her are decreasing, a woman may feel superfluous at times. The questioning process is underway. The questions come tumbling into her head and not always in logical order: How will she make the most of her new-found freedom? Does she wish to be a "lady of leisure"? Does she want to get her fill of travel? Now she has time to do some of these things she has always dreamed about but could never before fit into a tight schedule. Does she want to make music, pottery, or poems, design clothes, become a collector or a connoisseur, arrange flowers, ski to her heart's content, learn to fix cars, or take up a foreign language? Does she need to go back to school in pursuit of any of her goals or to complete an interrupted education? Is graduate school for her? Can she return to work without further training, or should she engage in some career-oriented or other volunteer work as a preparation for the years ahead? Will she need money, at least enough to cover her expenses? If she has a profession, does she want to return to that original profession? What are her alternatives now, or what will they be a few years from now when her family has grown up?

The more numerous the questions that pop up in her head, the more frightening the whole prospect becomes. A typical reaction to such fright is to push to whole idea aside, to hope that the sense of uneasiness and dissatisfaction with the status quo will go away like a bad dream. The temptation to procrastinate is therefore overwhelming. "Wait till after I get the house decorated." "Wait till after I get through with social obligations." There is always another "wait till after" lurking around the corner.

As experienced counselors of women know only too well, it takes great courage or great despair on the part of most women to make the first overt move. Perhaps my point is borne out best by the biographies in *Notable American Women, 1607–1950.** It seems that many of them had to overcome definite handicaps or difficulties, and often it was these very obstacles which drove them to success.

Fortunately, there are some practical ways to overcome this barrier: reading, using the worksheet as drawn up in Appendix B, and finally, availing yourself of counseling.

Reading. One of the first and easiest things which you can undertake on your own is to do some reading on the subject. Some suggestions can be found in the appendixes and in the bibliography.

It is not easy to make the transition from the generalities of the books to the specifics of one's own situation and to come to grips with one's own needs, hopes, or fears and the evaluation of one's skills.

From reading it will become evident even to the most tentative inquirer that there are certain basic questions which cannot be evaded. The simplest question of all is also the hardest to answer: "What do I really *want* to do?" as opposed to "What *should* I do?" Scrupulous honesty is in order here, requiring a rare knowledge of oneself, of one's capabilities, strengths, and weaknesses. How much, if any, training has atrophied? What new skills and expertise have been acquired in the interim? How have interests, ambitions, and expecta-

---

**Notable American Women, 1607-1950: A Biographical Dictionary*, edited by Edward T. and Janet W. James (Cambridge: Harvard University Press, Belknap Press, 1971).

tions changed? A woman must consider these things when she wishes to return to work, and she must think about them just as much if she decides in favor of volunteer work.

The Worksheet. A worksheet can be an invaluable tool for self-analysis. The one designed by Martha White and first published in *The Next Step** is an excellent example. Mary Albro, director of the vocational office of Smith College, helped me revise and update the worksheet for inclusion in this book.

Forcing oneself to sit down and make a self-evaluation, to state one's experience and goals *in writing*, is a cleansing process and an excellent exercise in discipline. It is both an enlightening and a discouraging experience.

Grappling with the worksheet is a very private matter. It can be done at home in unthreatening surroundings and is nobody else's business at this stage of the search. Exploration and discussion with the family come later. Husbands, in particular, can be of great support, or they may resent the whole idea.

Since the decision to undertake this exercise in self-evaluation involves no commitment to take action, there is no great fear of failure and hence no reason to put it off. The worksheet, sitting on top of the desk and challenging you to respond to its insistent questions, says, "Do it now!"

If done thoroughly, thoughtfully, and honestly, this important first step will make the next steps far easier and more productive. Once the problem areas are identified, it is comforting to discover a whole host of unexpected pluses. The balance sheet usually looks much more favorable than most women expect!

The Next Step, edited by Martha S. White, Mary D. Albro, and Alice B. Skinner (The Radcliffe Institute for Independent Study, 1964). Still available at the institute, 3 James Street, Cambridge, Massachusetts 02138.

This evaluation process cannot be rushed. If no other action is taken one can still benefit from updating the worksheet as personal circumstances change and new ideas take shape.

Counseling. Eventually the time will come when a woman feels ready to look into existing possibilities, and then there is no substitute for experienced, sympathetic, and well-informed counseling. At this crucial point a good counselor can help avoid much discouragment, disillusionment, and ultimate frustration and failure. I am in complete agreement with the statement in *The Next Step* that "the progressive steps of (1) determining interests, (2) analyzing marketable skills, and (3) arriving at a reasonable job objective are difficult to take without outside guidance and help."*

An experienced and knowledgeable counselor can provide invaluable assistance by knowing just how much to stimulate inquiry and imagination and how to channel the ideas once they start flowing. Too many ideas and alternatives can be as immobilizing as no ideas at all. The counselor can go over ground previously covered by the woman alone, be a sympathetic listener, and provide factual information.

A good counselor will also warn against the common pitfall of expecting too much too soon. Even the professional woman will find that she can rarely start exactly where she left off years ago; that she must not expect professional credit for fifteen years of maturing and experiences gathered in the meantime. Counselors who have watched other returnees begin again as "low woman on the totem pole" can assure an overeager client that this is often necessary and that she is not unique in her impetuousness. Intelligence, willingness to learn, and reliability are quickly detected in most organizations and businesses; and prompt promotion is likely. However, it is important to realize that overeagerness and

*White *et al.*, *op. cit.*, page 113.

ambition may mask a great deal of anxiety. Counselors of women agree that a disproportionately large part of their work goes into a steady building of morale which is often as important as the retraining of skills. Information on counseling as well as testing services can be found in Appendix A of this book.

Professional Women: Highly Trained Returnees
Highly trained professionals seem to have a psychological advantage at this point. They may have maintained contact with others in their field and thus may be more aware of suitable job openings. If a woman wishes to stay in her profession, her path may be clearly charted. The high degree of motivation that got her there in the first place most likely won't let her down now. This may apply to professional women such as architects, city planners, lawyers, librarians, management consultants, psychologists, teachers, and many others.* The more highly educated and trained a woman is, the more likely she will return to a paid position—and probably sooner than most. She has important things to do and has had years of study and training to learn how to do them. Chances are she is an extremely motivated person to begin with, and her drive to succeed is not going to desert her at this stage of her life. But she, too, should think long and hard and perhaps do some of the reading or even avail herself of counseling, as suggested for her less well-targeted sister.

Ten years ago, when a group of college presidents was worried about the high attrition rate of educated women from the labor market, they started "Catalyst" in New York, to provide counseling services for women anxious to stay in or return to work. The staff at Catalyst quickly had to revise its theory that most women who think they are ready to go to

*Refer to the redefinition of "professional" in Hilda Kahne's "Women in the Professions," *Journal of College Placement*, April-May 1973.

work need only a few helpful signposts to enable them to find their own way. Instead, they found just how frustrated and angry many of the women were who came for help. They also discovered how subjective the women were in their own estimation of their marketability. Felice N. Schwartz, Catalyst's president, confirms that women who have been out of the job market from ten to twenty years do indeed need help and guidance.

It is generally agreed then that housewifely activities tend to de-emphasize special skills, and foster self-deprecation and lack of confidence in dealing with the business or professional world on a competitive basis. This attitude, plus the tendency to take care of everybody else's needs first, can become habit-forming.

For the majority of women considering a return to work, some counseling is strongly recommended. Before the woman can actually start on a job successfully, she must deal with unrealistic expectations which may result in anxiety and low morale. Here is where a counselor can be most supportive.

Volunteer Work: A Bridge to the Work World

Good counselors will often suggest re-entry to the work world by way of volunteering. They may refer the client to one of many counseling and placement offices for volunteers.*

A woman would do well to become aware of some possible drawbacks before plunging into volunteer work. At first she will find herself getting out of social circulation during the daytime; but eventually her work during the day will also affect what she can do in the evening and on weekends. Her friends may write her off as unavailable for such things as going to a matinee or on a shopping spree, making up a women's double at tennis, playing golf, visiting the galleries,

*For full particulars see Chapter 16 and Appendix A.

joining an open house tour. These pleasures will still be possible in the future and are indeed one reason for choosing the more flexible schedule of a volunteer. Yet if she gets truly caught up in her work, her priorities will begin to shift. This is something most women realize only vaguely; it can become an irritation and a frustration particularly when "just a volunteer job" is standing in the way.

Profile of a "Returnee"—Volunteer. None of the latter considerations seem to trouble Mary Ellen: she has two children, sixteen and thirteen, and works almost full time as a volunteer. Her days and evenings are always busy, and to get her story I had to schedule an interview with her at 8 A.M. After graduating from high school she worked for eleven years as a receptionist for an optician. Her husband is an artist and teacher who inspired her to volunteer in the arts. She eventually became the head of volunteers at a contemporary art institute. She read a lot, helped at her church and her children's school, and discovered a real knack for understanding and working with adolescents. After a seminar in creative writing, she started writing regularly on her own. Her husband's sabbatical leave took the family to Italy for a year. Back home again, determined not to become "fossilized" at middle age, she readily accepted a call for help to run a state senatorial campaign and made a significant place for herself in local political affairs.

I just fell into place, skipping the difficult process of having to search and to present myself. Political work, on a personal local level, provides the kind of excitement I was seeking. I feel that the lack of a college degree has not hampered me at all in doing high-level volunteer work, and my husband gives me strong backing.

Mary Ellen has thought of getting some kind of paraprofessional training, an important, relatively novel alternative for noncollege-educated women like herself. She seems to be having such a good time in her varied volunteer activities, however, that these plans have not yet crystallized. Instead, she has decided to put her years of political volunteer work to the practical test and, after having run for office once, is now delving even more deeply into politics at the state level.

Profile of a Professional Woman Keeping Abreast of Developments in Her Field Through Volunteer Work. When Emily's three children were all enrolled in a summer camp for the first time, Emily, a trained psychiatric social worker, decided this was a golden opportunity to catch up on new developments in her field, particularly in group therapy. After graduating from social work school she had had four years of practical experience, which included the supervision of students. Emily worked right up to the birth of her oldest daughter thirteen years ago. Then she deliberately withdrew from her career, sensing that family and social work would draw on the same kinds of inner resources and that she could not do justice to both.

Her children are now seven, eleven, and thirteen years old; and Emily feels that bringing them up has definitely added to her professional awareness and competence. Certain professional skills have been enhanced by further experience with life, since her work is with people. For instance, she feels a greater sensitivity to the feelings and problems of others. She also has become more aware of her own ideas and has increased her ability to express them. On the minus side, however, she notes a certain loss of flexibility and desire to please and a tendency to get tired more easily.

Emily's request to find her a volunteer slot that could satisfy her particular wishes presented a challenge to our counseling staff. To everybody's delight, what seemed a most suitable opening at a psychiatric hospital came to our attention only a few weeks after Emily applied to us. Emily was referred to the volunteer director at that hospital. On closer scrutiny, the original proposal turned out to be unsuitable, but the resourceful volunteer director in turn referred Emily to the hospital's outpatient department, where the supervisor worked out a program that met Emily's specifications.

The staff respected Emily's professional credentials and accepted her offer to work with outpatients in group therapy. Emily herself was supervised by a senior social worker and a psychiatrist. She was also given the chance to become part of an in-take team, which sees patients both individually and in groups, and to take part in the follow-up diagnostic evaluation sessions.

Emily has kept up her work at the hospital throughout the year, three times a week. She relishes the freedom to choose what she most wants to do and enjoys the volunteer status too much to give it up at this time. Emily knows herself well and can gauge the amount of pressure she can tolerate and still function effectively at home and at work. She finds the time she now spends with her family has become more valuable to all of them. Flexible vacation scheduling is an important factor in her decision to remain a volunteer for at least another year, during which time she hopes to learn more about therapy with couples and develop more diagnostic skills.

For the moment Emily is not prepared to return to a paid position. She says she would feel compelled to do more than she can handle at present. If she were a salaried staff member, she would probably work more than originally anticipated and thus be prevented from spending needed time with the family.

Emily has deliberately left herself time for some of the fun things mentioned earlier. On the morning of our interview she was off to listen to a talk on landscape architecture, part of a special series which fascinated her.

12

The Volunteer-to-Career Concept

A woman may take up volunteer work with no other goal than to give service, or she may be planning from the outset to use volunteer work as a bridge to paid work.

No matter what the reason, though, she should choose her volunteer work with her goal clearly in mind and not just stumble into a volunteer situation. Volunteer jobs offer great learning opportunities if approached in the right spirit. With its flexible hours and a flexible vacation schedule, a volunteer job is well-suited to test one's interests and to try to determine how much extra work is compatible with already existing responsibilities.

In Washington, D.C., the Professional Center of the United States Employment Service assigned a staff interviewer to assist women who were seeking full- or preferably part-time jobs. Beginning in 1964, volunteer interviewers worked with the center's professionals in developing part-time employment opportunities. In 1966 the groups that had become involved in this project incorporated themselves as WOW (Washington Opportunities for Women),* and subsequently published a guide** modeled on *The Next Step.*

*WOW has opened up offices in six other cities.
**Washington Opportunities for Women, *A Guide to Part-Time Work and Study for the Educated Woman* (Washington, D.C.: Robert B. Luce, Inc., 1967).

It soon became apparent to the WOW group that "women may take a volunteer job with the express purpose of becoming visible and making contacts for a paid job." They also had to acknowledge the fact that there are "certain fields which offer the volunteer more variety and satisfaction than a paid job would." "In politics," they affirm, "volunteering is virtually the only way to begin."*

Members of WOW became so convinced that volunteer work must be considered as a possible and often promising approach toward a career that they organized a conference entitled "Volunteer to Career," held in Washington in October 1970. It was there that I first heard this concept expressed.

Return Engagement, published in 1970,** is a guide to part-time work and study in Philadelphia. The writers point out that "it is worth keeping in mind that the faithful experienced volunteer has an inside track when paid positions become available. Volunteering can be a gradual transition from the relative freedom of the home schedule for the demands of the working world. It offers a good opportunity to assess one's ability to juggle job and home responsibilities." In the section "How About a Volunteer Career?" women are advised to look into several volunteer assignments, judging them as carefully as they would any job offer.

Libby Welch, a women's employment counselor who directed her own agency for nearly a decade, maintains that, although volunteers may move up to paid positions, they must also realize that they can be passed over for the same reasons as any paid employee in a business organization.

---

*WOW *Guide*.

**Return Engagement*, edited by Carol Monnik Huth (Published by the Alumnae Associations of Barnard, Bryn Mawr, Mt. Holyoke, Radcliffe, Smith, Vassar, Wellesley, and the University of Pennsylvania Program for the Continuing Education of Women, 1971). Available from Bryn Mawr College, Bryn Mawr, Pennsylvania 19010.

Management may not consider an employee within the organization the most suitable one to promote and may prefer to bring in someone from the outside. When asked whether, in her opinion, volunteering in a business firm may be a possible route to a business career, Ms. Welch said that this is conceivable in a small firm, but she cautioned that such an unorthodox procedure would play havoc with personnel structure and employment practices in a larger firm. Her advice to women generally is to work for smaller firms, where she feels there is more variety and a better chance for recognition and promotion.

Certain counselors emphatically deny the potential of the "volunteer-to-career" approach for women. They maintain that it is hard, if not impossible, to find a paying job on the basis of a volunteer job well done. One of the reasons given is that uncommitted and unreliable volunteers have spoiled, and continue to spoil, the chances for others, for the new breed of volunteer professionals* who might very well reach their career goals through volunteering.

I have to concede that even though attitudes toward volunteers are changing, the change is indeed slow. It is not easy for some professionals to accept volunteers. Perhaps they feel threatened. Add to that the negative impact of volunteers who are working in jobs not suitable for them or who are not performing well, and one observes constant setbacks in the effort to improve the status of volunteers in the eyes of teachers, librarians, social workers, and others.

For the most part, though, my experience in Boston compares with that of the counselors in Washington and Philadelphia. In my work I have seen many examples of women who have moved from volunteer jobs to paid positions, whether within their own organization or elsewhere, on the strength of their volunteer experience.

*See Part One, Chapter 6.

Astute personnel managers check references rather thoroughly, especially when the supply of applicants is ample. They ask the opinion of an academic advisor just as readily as that of an applicant's immediate superior on a previous volunteer job.

Many people, and particularly women at this time, need the reassurance of their worth by monetary reward.

> *In the middle of the 1960s, one might have made an acceptable argument that money was losing its grip as the fundamental status medium. But this argument may not seem so sensible now. Then, one was struck by a sense of events departing from former patterns, and money-sensitivity may easily have been understood as one of the components left behind. But now, we are in what is, in part, an era of money. If the dollar is on its way out as a discipline, it is certainly making a flamboyant last stand.**

The necessity for that kind of recognition is still prevalent in our culture.

But there are those women volunteers who for a variety of reasons turn down a paying job when it is offered. Some wish to maintain a certain amount of independence of judgment and responsibility for the work in which they are engaged. This is certainly the view of Eleanor R. Searle, an active professional volunteer. She is a lobbyist for welfare agencies and organizations in Massachusetts and a member of the State Advisory Board for the Department of Public Welfare. She gained much of her specialized knowledge through her work with the League of Women Voters. She feels strongly that her volunteer status is crucial to her ability to lobby effectively. First, she has no personal economic stake in the decisions; and second, she is not tied by salary to any one agency or organization and thus can pick the issues she wishes to represent.

*Deckle McLean, *Boston Sunday Globe,* April 8, 1973.

For others there are highly complex personal reasons. For example, many women still do not wish to compete with men or are reluctant to become the chief wage earner in the family. For some women it is satisfaction enough to have had a salary offered them for the work they are performing as volunteers. I know of one highly competent professional volunteer who turned down the directorship of her agency, but asked that the offer be made to her in writing. She could foresee leaner years ahead and wanted to be armed with proof of her competence if she ever needed an income of her own.

The individual women whose experiences and interests are described in this chapter demonstrate much more than the drive to return to the work world via volunteering and further education. Each story tells of the struggle to decide how best to contribute talent and time, without sacrificing a family life pattern which took years to establish and without belittling the valuable experience gained in volunteering. Not all of the women succeeded in overcoming lack of self-confidence or low success expectations. Loosely grouped as "returnees," these women are particularly vulnerable to all the pressures against "making it" in a career; they are sensitive to these pressures and are articulate about reaching their goals.

Do some of the women who speak in this or other chapters sound too unusual, too exceptional? I am firmly convinced that there are few "usual" women, that each person is unique. Given the chance, a lot of encouragement, and some luck, women — if they persist — can successfully find their way into the work world. As the profiles in this chapter show, quite frequently volunteer or apprenticeship service is the bridge to the desired goal.

"The Delicate Balance" Between Home and Career
Vera, aged thirty-five and mother of two children (twelve and nine years old), has moved frequently.

Hers is a history of shifting from volunteer positions into paid ones. She says:

> *I have always tried to maintain a delicate balance between family and home and a career. Originally I was spurred by the loneliness and isolation of being a new mother. The first time I felt the need for a career or job was after the birth of my first child. Since my mother had never worked and had found fulfillment in the home and with various volunteer jobs, her female identity was a generation removed from mine. Thus, this was one of my first steps toward self-identity.*
>
> *Since taking this step many years ago, I have been fully gratified with my different jobs; yet thoughts keep trickling into my mind. I still find myself asking certain questions: How much energy do I want to give to a job? How much energy is taken away from family and home? Am I a career woman or a woman who spends her free time at an interesting job? Should I allot time to go away with my husband and thus remain in a low-keyed position where I am mobile and flexible? In short, what is the delicate balance and where is it for me and my growing family?*

Vera has become highly interested in the challenge of preserving the character of city neighborhoods. She currently holds a part-time paid job as environmental planner in a public planning agency where she started as a volunteer. She was trained on the job, considers herself "gainfully employed," and thoroughly enjoys her work. Yet her feelings about continuing graduate study in city planning at a leading design school (now possible on a part-time basis) are quite ambivalent. She rationalizes:

> *About further education — will the problems of the cities still be uppermost in my mind in ten years when I will have more time to devote? Going to school in city planning seems very specific and encroaches on my freedom of choice to work in other areas. The thought of fulfilling twenty courses for the requirement of a degree is a thought akin to prison. I feel I am still learning about the*

work of historic preservation, and if I were to choose school at this point it would be succumbing to fear of the future.

From Volunteer Apprenticeship to Gallery Director

Sonja came to our Volunteer Clearing House three years ago. She knew we had no paid jobs to offer, but realized that she would be wise to try an unconventional approach toward finding paid work. She badly needed money to help support a growing family and to meet some unusually heavy medical expenses. Having a discerning eye and a strong background in art history and liking to work with her hands, she immediately took to the suggestion that she might acquire a manual skill. The idea of learning everything about picture framing — learning to cut mats, to make wooden frames, to work with goldleaf, and to experiment with the latest materials (such as metal and Plexiglas) for picture framing — really appealed to her. After many telephone calls and personal visits and armed with a strong letter of introduction she managed to convince one of the more forward-looking frame shops in town to take her on as a "volunteer" apprentice.

It did not take long for the young owners of the frame shop to realize what a great find they had made. They soon offered to pay Sonja while still training her. In the beginning Sonja could work part-time only; sometimes she could not even come on her designated days. A very sick daughter at home required frequent and unexpected visits to the hospital for treatment, and there was nobody else to take the child but her mother. Sonja needed money to pay the doctor bills. But she also needed to get away from home during this difficult time, so that she could keep from becoming depressed. Through her work, she was able to bring home new enthusiasm.

Customers soon began to ask Sonja for ideas on how to frame their works of art. The store picked up more orders than they could handle, and although Sonja thoroughly enjoyed the actual work of framing, she soon became too valuable as a consultant and workshop manager to have time to use the matting knife and framing tools herself. The frame shop developed into a small gallery, where Sonja could use her knowledge of art to the fullest.

Today Sonja works almost full time and has become the gallery's director. Clients seek out Sonja's good judgment, knowledge, and taste; and they appreciate the personalized, reliable service they receive. An unorthodox way of using "volunteering"? Yes, but it worked beyond all expectation for this "returnee to work."

From Volunteer to the "First Woman Ever Hired for the Job"

Deborah is in her forties and the mother of two girls (eighteen and twenty) and a boy of ten. I visited her in her office near the State House, where she is one of three tax commissioners for the Commonwealth of Massachusetts. The other two are men, and she is the first woman ever to hold this position.

For many years she worked as a League of Women Voters member and taxation was her volunteer specialty. She became very knowledgeable in the field, lobbied, and wrote prolifically on the subject; and many professionals sought her advice. When she read in the paper that one of the tax commissioners was leaving, she applied for the job and was hired. She loves her work and puts in a full 9-5 day. Meanwhile, a friendly mother's helper welcomes her young son when he returns from school in the afternoon.

When we lunched in the state office cafeteria many "old pols" came over to speak to her. The exchange was always friendly and respectful. When I commented that she certainly was not anonymous, she replied that everyone knew who she was because she had visited their offices and introduced herself. She laughingly admitted that it was good for the ego and that she enjoyed her popularity.

Deborah obviously has lots of well-channeled energy. When her son was still a baby she decided to get a master's degree in philosophy and history, to complement her undergraduate major in economics. She found going back to school more difficult than her present full-time occupation. She has strong feelings about volunteer work. Convinced that it should involve the same kind of professionalism that a paid job requires in terms of commitment and intent, she is very much in agreement with the "volunteer professional" philosophy. With regard to part-time work for women she takes a rather independent and unpopular stand:

> *I think that unless women have specific skills or talents which justify such an arrangement they ought not to assume that they are automatically entitled to part-time employment. It is my opinion that given the present system, if women want to work they must be prepared to do so on a professional and competitive basis.*

"Volunteer-to-Career" and Further Education

There are those women who, after doing volunteer work for a while, become highly interested in a specific area and decide that they need to learn more about it. These women return to school for additional in-depth training to qualify themselves for a career.

Then there are also women who, intending to continue with graduate studies after their family responsibilities have lessened or altered, find volunteer jobs a useful way to maintain or to learn disciplines in the interim.

Settling on a Specific Career After Experimenting as a Volunteer. Barbara's three children are almost on their own now. But two children in college and uncertain conditions in her husband's business make it mandatory that Barbara soon contribute to the family's total income. She has a solid background in home economics, with years of family-related volunteer experience; and she has done extensive volunteer work with foreign students. Barbara really became serious about a professional career while serving as a school volunteer in Connecticut; she found that intensive tutoring of two elementary school students made a big contribution to their academic success and had a positive effect on the lives of their families. Her unusual patience and deep understanding of and sympathy for children made her a highly successful tutor, and she thoroughly enjoyed the training and supervision she received as a "school volunteer."

While working she began to read widely in the field of education and was pleased to find her mind as active as ever, rediscovering old academic habits. She was accepted for graduate study in "learning disabilities" at a teacher-training college, which allowed her to complete the course and obtain her degree at her own pace.

Even though there is an overabundance of teachers at the moment, there is a steady demand for persons with Barbara's specialty, training, life experience, and temperament. At present she is still student-teaching, but a permanent job is already waiting in the wings.

What is more, not wanting to be outdone by his mother, one of her children decided to return to school and finish his interrupted college career.

Volunteer-to-Career in Practical Politics Combined with Teaching. Marge says:

For the last six years I have been working in politics. My earlier working experience was in advertising and promotion.

My political volunteer jobs have included making convention arrangements for a candidate for state attorney general, organizing part of a district for a congressional candidate, and working with a partner in the state headquarters of the McCarthy-for-President Campaign in 1968.

At that point I felt the need to know more about the day-to-day mechanics of state government and volunteered one day a week in the State House. This volunteer job so increased in scope that I asked to be put on the payroll, and began working three days a week. My other political activities have been more education-oriented: I have taught political seminars both to undergraduates and continuing-education students. This year I am going back to school myself.

During this six-year period, while my own involvement has increased, my husband has also had a career change, resulting in a freer time schedule for him in the winter months. Thus we have been able to share the housework and child care and both contribute to our family's financial support. But we have run into a serious and unexpected snag with this arrangement: we are seldom at home at the same time. Just when I am free to take over in the house, he often has to leave (and vice versa)! In spite of this difficulty and the problems of bringing up our active and vocal children, we are generally pleased with the way we live.

A Returnee Who Volunteers and Goes to School. Ginny is a returnee whose experience parallels that of the college undergraduate — volunteer work contributed significantly to her understanding and enjoyment of academic courses.

Ginny got married after her junior year in college. Four children and ten years later she began to take courses for credit toward her bachelor's degree. Now she expects to go on to graduate school. Her special area of interest is family studies, including child development and parent-child relationships. She expresses herself forcefully:

Since my original major was English literature (and I had thought of continuing in this area), it came as a revelation to me that I could apply what I was learning. I could visualize a face, an action, or a relationship to give meaning to the information I was acquiring. This realization became my rationale for volunteering. After many years of schooling stressing the abstract, I was amazed at the increased interest which I felt by combining practical and intellectual stimuli. Although this type of dual perspective might be unnecessary or difficult in some academic areas, its inclusion in the field of human relations would seem to be imperative, though often strangely neglected. From a personal point of view, both the search for *and the* involvement with *volunteer work help to clarify career objectives. I discovered my abilities and limitations as well as my preferences and dislikes. This is particularly true for the student who returns to academics after many years. My confidence was restored by feeling useful and by associating with others at many levels, from professionals to children in need.*

Volunteer activity helps to dispel that feeling of restlessness which comes from sitting in a library thinking and reading about everything that needs to be learned. A persistent curiosity impels me, periodically, to become involved and to see for myself.

The reality can be so different from the imagined, which is inevitably clouded by preconceptions. Without this experience, there is the danger of overintellectualization, and there is a sense of something missed, as if the periphery had been fully explored while the heart of the matter remains obscure. Even a partial glimpse into this obscurity is revealing, and adds enormously to both interest and understanding.

Clearly, I am using volunteerism *as a means to an end. This does not diminish its importance for me, but emphasizes its flexibility. It is a marvelous way to broaden perspectives, to form new theories or test old ones, and to plan realistically for the future while enjoying an exposure to lives in progress.*

Erasing the Line Between Volunteering and Professionalism. Alice Warner is a woman who has come full circle. Her long volunteer experience extends, through further education, right back to a professional commitment to the area of volunteering itself.

Alice has volunteered in many capacities over the past two decades. During the '60s, while her children were all in school, her interest focused on public school libraries. She helped organize and run several in her own community, and later became part of a volunteer team setting up school libraries in Boston. Gradually, thanks in large part to volunteers like Alice, these libraries have been turned over to long-needed professional school librarians. With family

responsibilities decreasing, she returned to college to become a professional librarian herself. Not unreasonably, one of her primary professional interests is the role of the volunteer in American libraries. Her published research on volunteers within a professional setting reveals that libraries and library training schools still are not facing this issue squarely. In a recent *Library Journal* article, she corroborates my remarks about the status of volunteers and the antagonism that some volunteer-professionals face in fields such as teaching and social work:

> *. . . Are students in library schools today in the U.S. and Canada being made aware of voluntarism as a continuing force? Are their roles as library professionals in this movement being analyzed, clarified, discussed? Are they learning how to become trainers of helpers, how to become trainers of trainers?*
>
> *It is my impression that many professional people in the library field are understandably nervous and negative when the word "volunteers" is mentioned. . . . There is concern over loss of jobs, there are troubled thoughts about "professionalism" and "protection," "status," and "standards." There is a strong feeling of "just as we're getting on our feet professionally, the volunteers take over . . ."**

Her findings provide convincing evidence that there is a need for extended professional training at the library-school level. By further developing volunteer resources, both the libraries and the communities they serve will benefit. Alice goes on to say:

> *Many professional librarians and local teachers of library science feel, most understandably, that the very existence of these volunteers prevents the development of paid library positions; they feel that only people with library-school training can run these libraries properly. In the latter surmise they are undoubtedly right; a*

*Alice Sizer Warner, "Voluntarism and Librarianship," *Library Journal*, April 1, 1972, pp. 1241-1245.

person depth-trained in library skills and philosophy would be ideal for these enterprises, especially if he were a native of the community in question. If the librarian's background, ideals, and vocabulary were different from those of the library's community, however, ideally community aides should also be present to provide the needed ethnic bridge. A busy library can absorb any number of helping hands. . . .

Alice's loyalty and concern for volunteering have persisted, even though she is now a qualified professional with a "career." Her experience shows that the dividing line between volunteering and professionalism can be successfully erased by strong personal commitment.

13

Women Alone

One outcome of the feminist movement to date is the public's greater awareness of the large number of "women alone." Single women, widows, and divorced women have a peculiarly undefined and amorphous role in our society. These women are becoming increasingly conscious of the fact that they can expect little outside support, whether emotional, structural, or financial; they must function without much attention from the world of the "marrieds."

Single women — women who have never married, will probably never marry, or are determined not to marry—are known by many derogatory names: spinsters, bachelor girls, old maids, to give a few. Even the word "single" itself often evokes a negative image in the public's mind: something is wrong, something is missing. Yet today, more and more women are deliberately staying single or choosing nonpermanent relationships.

Out of the more than twelve million people in America who are *widowed*, ten million are women. In more striking terms, on the average a married woman can expect to be a widow for eight years.* As widows, these women must grapple with a set

*"Volunteer Community Work," by Chase Going Woodhouse, in *American Women: The Changing Image*, edited by Beverly Benner Cassara (Boston: Beacon Press, 1962), pp. 50 ff.

of unique problems.

It seems to me that of the identifiable "legal" categories of women, *divorced* women are the most difficult to classify as a group. The variety of individual circumstances, especially the wide range of ages, may mask one thing these women have, or have had, in common: a certain sense of guilt or failure. Before these women can deal with the prejudice and hostility which they are likely to encounter, they must first come to terms with themselves.

As a rule, "women alone" are the *least likely* candidates for volunteer jobs. Practical and financial considerations, as well as the psychological problems of being alone in a society designed for couples, can make volunteering difficult.

It is not a coincidence that in the existing literature about single women I have found only the most superficial references to volunteer work. Volunteer service is rarely mentioned as a possibility to help ease the loneliness which so often goes with being single. Nevertheless, it is my experience that some women alone *do* find important personal satisfaction through volunteer work.

A new magazine, *Single*, purports to

> reach individuals who by choice or by chance find themselves single in a marriage-oriented society . . . help them to adjust, to develop fully, to discover identity, to enhance self-esteem, to learn how to relate to others, to find love, work, and discover a new sense of worth.*

(I trust that the definition of work includes volunteer as well as paying positions, for both are capable of helping people to achieve that goal.)

Out of all the "women alone," single women are the ones who most consistently find volunteering an attractive alterna-

Single, a magazine for the unmarried, divorced, widowed, and unattached, August 1973.

tive. If they are working women, as is often the case, they will probably choose evening or weekend volunteer work.

Many of the profiles already presented are those of single women, giving of themselves and of their time . . . people helping people.*

The Widow

The woman who finds herself uncoupled by circumstances or by design is less likely to volunteer than the single woman. Yet there are exceptions. This section on the widow begins by exploring her status in our society and describes some self-support schemes. Then follow a few examples of widows who have had successful volunteer experiences or who see in voluntary service a means to find new direction.

Unfortunately, a widow cannot expect much help and support from a society that finds death uncomfortable and painful to deal with, if not downright threatening. "The comfort of the clergy and the funeral director, family and friends, soon fades. All about there is the expectation to keep a stiff upper lip."** Family and friends will assist to the best of their ability — an ability that varies greatly. Often after a brief time the new widow is on her own, and must find inner resources to help her adjust to her new status.

"In a world of couples, one is half of a team."*** The widow has to learn to live with the stigma of being single. Suddenly she has to make all of the decisions. There is no partner with whom to discuss problems and search for solutions. She alone bears the entire responsibility, and small tasks tend to get blown out of proportion.

Columnist Joan Millman goes on to say:

*See for example Part Two, Chapters 7-9, 12.
**Joan Millman, "Carry On," in *Boston Sunday Globe,* July 16, 1972.
***Ibid.

Studies have shown that the bereaved are more vulnerable to mental illness, physical disorder, suicide, alcoholism, drug addiction, and early death. The death of a spouse is for most people a traumatic experience that produces drastic changes in every aspect of life. At the core is the problem of new identity, the role of "widow," and the attendant myths, attitudes, and behavioral expectations society imposes. Psychiatrists agree that the road back depends upon the realistic acceptance of death. The trajectory of grief passes through the stages of "impact," when the subject is stunned and in shock; "recoil" when full awareness occurs and the most stress is experienced; and "recovery" when reintegration of the new status takes place.

This cycle takes time and must be allowed to run its natural course.

Widow-to-Widow Project. Recognizing the special needs of the newly bereaved, Dr. Gerald Caplan and Dr. Phyllis Silverman, two members of the Community Psychiatry Department of the Harvard Medical School, started the "Widow-to-Widow Project" in 1967. Plans to spread the program nationally are underway.*

The "Widow-to-Widow Project" recruited as its volunteers widowed women who themselves had worked through many of the problems described above. Contacts with newly bereaved women were made through the clergy, funeral homes, mental health centers, and friends. Trained volunteers, with a deep understanding of the problems born of their own experiences, were able to provide support to the newly bereaved as few others could.

A "Widowed Service Line" is one possible outgrowth of the Widow-to-Widow Project. Such a 24-hour telephone answer-

---

*An excellent documentary and training film on the subject of widowhood (done in conjunction with the "Widow-to-Widow Project") has been produced by Dr. Edward Mason, a psychiatrist, and is available for rent through the Harvard Medical School.

ing service for widows was begun in Boston and was funded
by the National and Massachusetts Funeral Directors associations and the National Institute of Mental Health. This service
provides immediate and confidential contact for widows who
desperately want to talk to someone.

Widows are often hesitant to call upon friends and family
for extended help, counsel, and sympathy. Well-meaning
family members and friends may not be able to shoulder the
grief projected onto them and do not know how best to relieve
the depression of a person in mourning. Other people,
struggling to keep their immediate families intact, already
have their own problems. It is particularly difficult for men
and women in their middle years, who are already burdened
with many responsibilities, to provide the lifeline to which
the widow wishes to cling. The expectation of ready
understanding from friends and family easily turns into
resentment of apparent unfeelingness and lack of support.
The widow naturally assumes that no one can be suffering as
much as she.

All too frequently, loneliness, despondency, and a sense of
utter inadequacy accompany bereavement. Volunteers trained
to reach out to widows offer welcome relief. They can and will
make personal contacts, be patient listeners, help with solving
everyday problems, and know where to turn for assistance with
more complicated ones. They will try to include the widow in
some of their own social activities and generally be available
during "dark moods" and times of despair.

Rejoining Society. When the widow first feels a
desire to rejoin society, she needs strong support. This is the
time to venture out among friends and to make known her
intention of building a future life. If work of any kind is part of
these plans, friends and acquaintances can supply leads and
ideas.

It is also during this stage of recovery — as thoughts of re-entering the work world emerge — that suggestions of how to accomplish this transitional step are most helpful. More often than not, the economic situation demands that the widow find gainful employment as soon as possible; and she cannot afford the luxury of even an interim volunteer job. If the woman must also provide for children, she can hardly muster the extra energy for community work. She will need every ounce of her strength to keep functioning, to perform her job satisfactorily, and to continue to be available to her children.

If, on the other hand, financial conditions are such that it is feasible to start with a volunteer job, the transition may be more gradual . . . and less painful.

Volunteer-to-Career for a Widow. A Widow-to-Widow counselor referred Vivian to our Clearing House for volunteers. We had an opening for a paid secretary in our office, and although the available job did not seem commensurate with her abilities, Vivian decided to apply for it.

At the time of her visit, Vivian had been widowed for about two years and was holding a part-time paid research job. Unhappy with the limited scope that this job afforded her, and knowing that within a couple of years she would have to support herself entirely, Vivian was casting about for full-time possibilities.

We convinced her that instead of taking a full-time position with us, she should continue in her research job and at the same time work as a volunteer in our organization. She could see that the nature of our work would give her a good opportunity to survey the field and to explore various areas before making a more permanent decision.

Vivian treated her volunteer job in a most professional manner. Because she had an art background, her first assignment was to help a commercial artist design a brochure.

The professional designer accepted the volunteer's contribution, and Vivian had her first lesson in the economics of printing.

Since Vivian showed the tact and sensitivity needed to deal with people, she seemed a natural for counseling volunteers. We gave her full access to the resource files in our office, and soon she was familiar with the available volunteer opportunities. An experienced colleague was always at hand for assistance. Vivian began to observe counseling interviews until she felt ready to handle applicants by herself.

In order to get acquainted with the organizations to whom the Clearing House refers volunteers, Vivian made field visits; she wrote and filed a report after each one. As her self-confidence increased, she realized that she could handle all kinds of assignments.

Because of her volunteer work, life was a little less lonely for Vivian. She became a friend to us, and a full partner in the struggle of running a small, understaffed social service agency. We were able to convey to her that we needed her as much as she needed us. When the board chose her for the salaried position of director of the Independent Study Project for High School Seniors,* the fact that she was a widow never entered into the picture. Rather, she was selected in recognition of the outstanding ability she had demonstrated through volunteer work.

After a busy year as director, Vivian was appointed to a full-time executive position with one of Boston's major health agencies. Her greatest problem now is not knowing when to slow down.

A Son's Concern for his Widowed Mother. Recently a graduate student consulted us about his widowed

---

*See Part Two, "The High School Student," pp. 47-60, for a description of the program.

mother. After his father's death a year ago, John's mother, who had done volunteer work all her life, found it quite unbearable to go on with any of her accustomed activities. Her son was puzzled and deeply concerned:

> *I used to think of my mother as a super-volunteer, but when Dad died, nothing seemed to make sense to her any more. . . . Friends have been kind, but the invitations are beginning to taper off. Mother feels guilty about how little she herself did to include "single" women in our family's social life before my father's death. My teenage sister is quite shaken and seems threatened by Mother's apparent identity crisis. She and Mother are very much at odds. . . . I really feel I need to do something. . . .*

Most likely Mrs. T will not return to her previous rather conventional volunteer activities. Having become painfully aware of the delicate web of personal interrelationships based on the assumption of a society of couples, she may now be receptive to new ideas and a completely different type of volunteer role. John realizes that his mother's relative material comfort is almost destructive, in that it allows her to be paralyzed in inaction. He would like to see her redirect her energies into more challenging volunteer activities.

There is no "Friendly Visitor" hotline or Widow-to-Widow project in Mrs. T's community. John feels that because of her extensive volunteer experience, his mother could be the initiator and organizer of such a venture.

The Volunteer Grandmother. Another kind of request came to me from a woman who had lost her husband and subsequently took over his business. Her upbringing and previous life experience had prepared her better than most women to be successful as head of the firm. Yet soon the strain began to tell. While Ina found herself becoming highly efficient, she was alarmed at sensing a certain loss of patience and warmth. Her children were in their teens, and she did not want to become a callous or harsh mother.

Ina had always been very fond of infants and had a special knack in caring for them. When she came to our office, she specifically requested that we find her a volunteer placement which would allow her to work with very young children once or twice a week. "Where can I be most useful in the limited time I can take off during business hours?" she asked.

Since Ina wanted an institutional setting, a hospital pediatric ward was the obvious spot. We told her that the city hospital desperately needed help, but that paradoxically the severe staff shortage there made good supervision difficult, causing a constant turnover of discouraged volunteers.

Because of her common sense and initiative, Ina could cope with the fact that some days there was a surplus of volunteers on the floor, while at other times no one was around to comfort a crying baby. She could see for herself what needed to be done, and did not have to depend on explicit instructions.

Ina looked forward to her days at the hospital and got a great deal of pleasure out of working with very young pediatric patients and their parents. She kept up the habit for years, until her daughter had children. Now she has become a genuine after-hours and weekend grandmother!

Divorced Women

On a nationwide basis, nearly half of all marriages will end in divorce. This rapid increase in the incidence of divorce has overwhelmed existing social and legal institutions. The fact that, according to *Marriage: Trends and Characteristics* (U.S. Department of Health, Education, and Welfare, Publication No. 72-1007), less than 50 percent of divorced women over twenty-five will ever remarry means that large numbers of "women alone" are divorced women.

Like widows, many divorced women suffer from loneliness and a loss of moral and financial support. Whereas at one time these women had been dependent on another person for security, they may now begin to question their own sense of worth. As a result of their new status within our "coupled society," both widows and divorced women tend to be forced out of their previous social networks. Some of these women may even choose to withdraw from their former friends and activities, not wanting to face rejection.

Unlike the widow, whose fate evokes pity and compassion, the divorced woman often faces animosity and jealousy. Society puts her on the defensive. Because of their own insecurities, married friends may perceive her as a menace. Wives often suspect a divorced woman's motives. They may also fear that a woman who appears to be making it on her own holds a certain attraction for their husbands.

The divorced woman is set apart from other "women alone" in that she is likely to experience a sense of personal failure caused by an unsuccessful marriage. Especially when there are children, feelings of guilt add further complications. The woman is almost sure to feel that in some way she has let down those she loves most.

Many women are vocationally unprepared, socially isolated, and emotionally vulnerable. They are often ill-equipped for the realities of divorce. Divorce raises basic questions of self-identity. Even though the stigma of divorce is no longer as damaging as in the past, separation is always a disorganizing experience. For some women, divorce brings a sense of relief; for others, only distress. In either case, after an initial period of readjustment, the divorced woman must learn to cope and begin to reconstruct her life. As Judith Bardwick argues, "The loss of sources of self-esteem and criteria of identity have to be replaced, and new tasks evolved in order to experience a feeling of growing, living, being."*

*Judith Bardwick, *Psychology of Women: A Study of Bio-Cultural Conflicts* (New York: Harper and Row, 1971), p. 216.

My experience indicates that women who are divorced or separated are unlikely to use volunteer work to fulfill such needs. In no other group is it brought home so forcefully and so brutally that women are still financially dependent on men. Only in those rare cases where adequate provision is made, either through divorce settlement or thanks to an independent income, does there exist an either/or choice between volunteer and paid work. Usually it is a top priority for the divorced woman to supplement her income—a struggle that becomes more complicated when children are involved. If children remain with the mother, as is still the customary arrangement, her energies must be focused on an income-producing job. Juggling the responsibilities of "single head of household" and making seemingly endless care-taking arrangements for the children generally preclude volunteer activities.

Some divorced women have formed self-help groups to assist others during the initial trauma of separation and to

help them deal with the consequences of divorce. "Justice for Divorced and Separated Mothers," a voluntary action group, was started by several young mothers a few years after their own divorces.

These women are in a position to understand first hand the problems of persons in similar situations. They now realize that they should have been better informed and advised before their divorces. Most never really understood the long-term effects of divorce. They did not anticipate the consequences in human terms or the pitfalls inherent in arrangements for custody, child support, child care, and visitation.

In an attempt to keep other women from making the same mistakes, "Justice for Divorced and Separated Mothers" hopes to:

—provide services designed to meet immediate needs for information and support;
—facilitate communication between the community, existing institutions, and members and point out the actual and acute needs of divorced and divorcing mothers;
—provide women with opportunities which will ultimately enable them to achieve self-realization in terms of family living and employment.*

The volunteers are convinced that all self-help organizations must provide for the active participation of members in all phases of the program, from the initial planning to the execution and follow-up.

Members of "Justice for Divorced and Separated Mothers" realize that competent legal counsel is costly, and that many women simply cannot afford a good lawyer to arrange equitable divorce or separation agreements. Furthermore, when these agreements are not adhered to, legal help

*A funding proposal submitted by Justice for Divorced and Separated Mothers, Inc.

becomes essential. Child support, especially when the father moves out of state, is often a major point of contention. The organizers believe that there is much preventative and support work that nonlawyers can do to help women prepare divorce proceedings.

Hoping to end the unpleasantness of the present "system of accusation," with its "almost-required perjury,"* many other groups now sponsor no-fault divorce. They further maintain that full disclosure of both the husband's and wife's financial holdings would reduce legal work.

While I feel that volunteering can offer divorced women an important emotional outlet and help them meet new people, experience shows that the majority of them tend to shy away from such commitments, at least in the beginning. Many women faced with separation even give up volunteer work they had been doing previously. They are unwilling to face people with whom they formerly associated and wish to avoid the inevitable questions — whether voiced or implied.

Nevertheless, volunteering can fit into the planned routine of the "woman alone" and help fill much empty time, particularly in the evening and on weekends. Without claiming that volunteering is an ideal solution for divorced women, I would like to present two profiles of divorced women who have used volunteering for their purposes.

Volunteering Before and After Divorce. Barbara, an administrative assistant, writes from Delaware:

> *When I was married, I helped in an election campaign and thought about social service volunteer work, but after my divorce I was always busy earning a living and coping with house and home. For a while, I did volunteer in a community theater group, but my motivations for giving my time were entirely selfish; theater*

---

*Norman Sheresky and Marya Mannes, *Uncoupling: The Art of Coming Apart* (New York: Viking Press, 1972).

work has always been a great love of mine, and basically I am a ham at heart.

Recently, I took the step into real *volunteer service. With my boss's semi-retirement, my regular job became less demanding. I was totally isolated in my office 'way out in the country. I saw no one all day, and didn't have enough to keep me busy. As an "unremarried woman," I needed contact with people. I wanted a challenge and sought to put my skills to use where there was a need.*

Now I work like a dog on the two afternoons I spend each week at the prison where I volunteer. Last month I was even put on a committee to improve relations between volunteers and staff, quite a delicate task. My motives are by no means completely altruistic; I am not out to help mankind, but rather to help me be a happier, less lonely person. If I can also make a few of the prisoners feel that someone cares about them, so much the better.

After next year I will be able to afford six months off, and hope to live and work in England. On my return I will have to be somewhat concerned with old age security and either find a job with a pension plan or else with a terrific salary so that I can create my own. In either case, I shall insist that there be enough time for me to continue my volunteer work at the prison.

Under today's system, the process of divorce can take many months. This period, often an unpleasant time of anxious waiting and negotiating, can be very trying for all parties involved.

One divorced woman decided not to let this difficult time get her down. While filing for a divorce in Reno, Tara began to feel the strain of the entire procedure. After some hesitation, she contacted the local YWCA to see if there was anything she could do while she was waiting around town. Sure enough, they needed a swimming instructor; and Tara, a former lifeguard, filled the bill. Being able to do something she enjoyed helped to pass the time during her divorce hearings. She liked this job so much that when she came home after her divorce became final, she began giving swimming lessons on a part-time basis at her local Y.

During the first period after the loss of their partner, when problems of trauma and crisis are dominant, the separated and the widowed are apt to define themselves as having little in common. Widows are likely to resent being grouped together with "divorcees." With the passage of time, however, the separated and the widowed find their problems more nearly alike.*

All "women alone" share certain characteristics. Yet single women, widows, and divorced women often differ in their reactions to aloneness. That reaction, in turn, influences the extent to which voluntarism can affect these women's lives.

*Robert S. Weiss, *The Contributions of an Organization of Single Parents to the Well-Being of Its Members* (Cambridge: Laboratory of Community Psychiatry, Harvard Medical School, 1972).

14

Retirees and Preretirees

If volunteering has been part of the pattern of one's life, it is easy to stay involved in service to others after retirement. But persons who have not been volunteers before retiring don't automatically feel the urge to begin.

One of the nation's leading electronics companies conducts a series of workshops for their employees scheduled to retire. For several years I have been involved with the program as it touches upon volunteering and explores volunteer opportunities for "after retirement." Our staff has continuously been available for counseling and placement, but so far the workshop participants' response has been minimal. Occasionally an enterprising wife takes up the offer of assistance for herself. More often, it is the women who make tentative inquiries on behalf of their husbands, so soon to be out of work and presumably around the house for most of the day. Fearful of what this drastic change may mean to the family, the wives wish to prepare for that moment, hoping to ease the adjustment.

On the other hand, there are couples who have made plans years in advance and can hardly wait to carry them out. For a few that means a move to another part of the country or even to another continent. Sometimes women faced with retirement are more willing to make a big move, perhaps to join children or relatives elsewhere. But for the majority of

Americans, retirement simply means having more time on one's hands.

For some there is always the chance of starting that second career in the capacity of "volunteer professional."

In the section on "Talent Pools" in Part Three, Chapter 16, I describe in some detail what the members of a senior center in Winnetka, Illinois, decided to do with their enforced leisure time. These people, retired professionals and business executives, were convinced that their skills should not go unused, and they created a highly successful volunteer skills bank which has served as a model for others.

An impressive number of retirees from the world of education and social work merely "switch hats" when that arbitrary retirement date arrives. While it is true that a few find paid work in their fields or are hired as consultants, most of them have to make the transition from paid professional to volunteer professional. For the time being, younger men and women are waiting to seize the available paid positions, leaving few such opportunities for their seniors.

Upon retiring, the former head social worker of a Family Service agency took a four-week vacation with her husband. She then reported for work as a "volunteer" supervisor of volunteer case-aides assigned to inner-city families. Only an "old pro" could give these carefully selected, well-intentioned volunteers the training and supervision necessary to make such a bold, all-volunteer social-work project function. In a way, therefore, the number of volunteers that can successfully be enrolled is often limited by the availability of volunteer professionals to supervise them.

Another ex-social worker whose interest in people is as keen as ever chose to become a volunteer interviewer for the local Voluntary Action Center. Always short of help, the center's staff is delighted to benefit from Evelyn's enthusiasm, knowledge of resources, and great gift for relating to people anxious to offer their volunteer services.

One retired headmistress of a private girls' school is learning what it is like to teach in a crowded urban elementary school. Working as a school volunteer, she feels a new sense of accomplishment. But she has had to make major adjustments, and her ideas on education have received quite a jolt. She has been compelled to revise some of her long-held beliefs on *How Children Fail.**

These examples of active, alive, and concerned "retired" citizens confirm my belief that a life experience of reaching out to others leads to continued active participation in the affairs of the world. Keeping busy lets one forget aches and pains. It also helps to know that somebody needs you and that you can be of help to others. With so much to do, there is not enough time to feel useless.

As previously mentioned, developing such attitudes early in life is becoming far more commonplace. Still, no one should be discouraged from starting at any time; it is really never too late to try, especially with sympathetic support. The tradition of voluntary service is strong in this country, and visitors from abroad never cease to marvel at its scope. Yet many women and men in their sixties remain untouched by the volunteer spirit; would that they were flexible enough to open themselves to a totally new experience!

"Senior Power" is a catchy slogan, but to translate it into a vital force will require education and a profound change of attitudes. Easy acceptance of obsolescence is built into American society, whether it relates to goods or people. Marya Mannes's nightmarish fantasies in her book *They*** of what could happen if obsolescence with respect to people were carried to its ultimate degree must not become reality. "They" — the older generation — must not be placed in total isolation and left to deteriorate through sheer useless-

*John Holt, *How Children Fail* (New York: Pittman Publishing Co., 1964).
**Marya Mannes, *They* (Garden City: Doubleday & Co., Inc., 1968).

ness. Perhaps the hotly debated issue of the "generation gap" has made us temporarily lose sight of what older people can contribute to society.

A Retired Couple

Within the last few months I have made the acquaintance of a married couple who retired from a jointly managed store in the Middle West. Their dream was to travel and be free of obligations. They sold their house, bought a camper, and toured first this country and then south of the border. But they soon began to feel at loose ends. They missed not having any obligations to others — obligations which had overwhelmed them at their former home. So they decided to settle in the South, and, notwithstanding Mr. D's heart condition, both husband and wife have chosen to work regularly at a local day-care center. They each give two days a week: one day each works alone and once a week they work together on the same day, thus sharing some of their experience, comparing notes, and providing a completely new interest in their greatly changed lives. A recent visit to relatives was cut short, because their "vacation" was over, and duty and their young charges at the day-care center were calling them back to their new life.

A Retired Man

Frank commuted daily from his home to his job in the trust division of a bank. When his turn for retirement came, he chose to make the accustomed commute once a week to work as a volunteer in one of the social agencies on whose board he serves as treasurer. He looks forward to his workday in the city. He makes up the payroll, keeps the agency's books, prepares the monthly and annual balance sheets, arranges for audits, tax payments, etc., and comes up with ideas for a more streamlined operation. If he misses the plush surroundings and the secretarial services he was used to in his bank job, he does not show it. Instead, he seems to enjoy the rather informal atmosphere of the agency's office and is fascinated by the variety of people who come to it. For lunch he usually has a date with his friends and colleagues from the bank, just a block away. The agency has never had such expert professional help before, and Frank is left in no doubt as to how much his volunteer service is appreciated.

Volunteering by the Elderly: Government Programs

Some new programs are emerging which attempt to make constructive use of the vast reservoir of talent, energy, and experience of the elderly. The federal "Foster Grandparent Program" has been in operation since 1965. Carefully selected low-income senior citizens are encouraged to work with institutionalized children whose families cannot cope with them at home. Areas of work include pediatric wards, homes for dependent and deprived children, and institutions for the mentally retarded, the emotionally disturbed, and the physically handicapped. In the past, at least, the federal government provided subsidies for transportation and some other compensation for the volunteers. Yet no one can estimate the value in dollars and cents of the immense patience and the gifts of time, kindness, and warmth which these senior citizens bring to the isolated and sometimes forgotten children who live in institutions year round.

One would hope that the funding of so successful a program will continue. However, programs seem to come and go, depending on who writes the most persuasive proposal for yet another "pilot project" to attract financial backing.

RSVP (Retired Senior Volunteer Program) was begun in 1969 under the auspices of the U.S. Department of Health, Education, and Welfare. Its aim is to encourage senior citizens to do volunteer work and to find suitable placements for them.

In 1964 the Small Business Administration established SCORE (the Service Corps of Retired Executives) for men and women who wish to volunteer their expertise in small business administration and can give help with operating and management problems.

Both of these programs now come under the umbrella of ACTION, the government agency currently responsible for all voluntary action programs, including the Peace Corps and VISTA. ACTION has ten regional offices throughout the country.

Yet, the federal government need not be the impetus for all senior citizen projects. Volunteers staff a tourist information center at the State House in Boston. Most of these volunteers are retired men and women, eager themselves to learn more about their city and New England in general. They thoroughly enjoy the contact with the public and are happy to pass on their knowledge to out-of-town or foreign visitors. Working in pairs, the volunteers often develop new friendships. They eagerly look forward to their tour of duty of two to four hours per week. This regular assignment brings them out of the isolation of their homes, and lets them play a part in the life of the city.

Even New England winters do not seem to dampen their enthusiasm. Bad weather may discourage tourists, but except for a bona fide case of flu it rarely keeps the senior volunteer information officers away from the job. Perhaps one of the most faithful of them all is a man of 73, a former securities salesman, who lives alone and thrives on the new contacts he makes each week while manning the information desk. Reduced subway and busfares help to make volunteer service financially feasible for persons over 65.

Lists of volunteer opportunities particularly suited for older people should be available at volunteer bureaus throughout the country (see Part Three, Chapter 16, "How to Locate a Suitable Volunteer Job"). For this group of potential volun-

teers, it is of the utmost importance to have easy access to the place of work. Unfortunately, in recent years the safety of getting to and from the volunteer job has also become a major consideration. That factor alone can influence the availability of volunteers. Thus, recognizing this problem, the National School Volunteer Program has used funds available for the elderly to bus them to and from the public schools in much the same way as some of the city children in whose schools they work as volunteers. Making the trip safe for the elderly has, in turn, brought many more senior citizens into the school volunteer programs—to such an extent that it has subtly changed the character of these programs in some large cities.

Preretirement

Retirement seems to come earlier than in the past to greater numbers of men and women. Mr. S was sent to us for advice and suggestions by his wife, a dietitian, who herself had obtained a volunteer position in a community health outreach program. Mr. S had done well in business and did not need to augment his income. Yet—at 55—he was not prepared to stop "working." He made it quite clear that his outdoor interests would keep him busy enough in the summer, but that he needed a full-time occupation during the rest of the year. After much discussion, he narrowed his choice to three possibilities, all of which he carefully investigated in person. He considered working as a research assistant and aide to a prominent politician; he turned down an offer to be a consultant to minority businesses (he really did not want a busman's holiday in preretirement); and he finally elected to work at the Museum of Science as "Jack-of-all-trades" five days a week. Both parties report that they are extremely pleased with the experiment.

Volunteering Helps Bridge the Generation Gap

Regardless of age, people can start volunteer projects on their own.* A twelve-year-old entrepreneur started a "Rent-a-Plant" business with his grandfather.

Not everyone has a green thumb. Some people are incapable of growing anything, but almost everybody loves plants. Jonathan and his grandfather tend their homemade greenhouse and rent out plants for fifty cents a month. At the end of that time, they call to check on the plants, pick them

---

*Other examples of "Take-charge projects" are suggested in Part Three, Chapter 17.

up, or replace them. So far the gasoline shortage has not forced them out of business. Almost all of the money they collect goes into equipment, tools, and fertilizer, barely covering operating expenses. At home they also take care of the plants of customers going on vacation. They accept no fee for this "plant-sitting" service, asking only for a cutting from each plant; they maintain their pinching rights! Plants could be rented to nursing homes, to schools, or to shut-ins. If delivery and transportation are difficult for an older person, particularly during inclement weather, the young volunteer can help with that chore.

Such teamwork has obvious additional benefits for both the older and the younger partner. A little imagination will go a long way, and there is no "patent applied for" restriction on imitating successful volunteer projects.*

*The Clearinghouse of the Voluntary Action Center in Washington, D.C., has compiled and indexed many other "do-it-yourself" volunteer projects, which may be obtained from The National Center for Voluntary Action, 1625 Massachusetts Avenue, N.W., Washington, D.C. 20036.

15

The Newcomer to Town

Frequent moves and constant uprooting characterize today's mobile society. Thousands of Americans pick up stakes each year: people change jobs, students go away to school, the adventuresome wish to try living in different parts of the country, corporations shift their executives from place to place. As a result, many communities experience a flux in population; a steady stream of newcomers filters into town. There are major and minor challenges that go with settling into a new community. Can newcomers and existing community institutions find constructive methods of adapting to each other? One way for new arrivals to integrate themselves better into their new surroundings is to participate in certain volunteer activities, or to join a voluntary organization or two.

Along with the "Welcome Wagon," which combines a mercantile interest with its hospitality, church- or school-related community organizations often provide a first welcome. One group that offers special assistance to newcomers is FISH, an acronym for Friendly Immediate Sympathetic Help. Originally begun in England, this group has adopted the symbol by which early Christians identified each other. Today's members still identify themselves with a picture of a fish in the window. They describe themselves as "a group of untrained, ordinary people who feel the need to express their love and concern for their neighbors." All of the services are offered by people in their spare time and include such things as emergency transportation, child care, and companionship for shut-ins, as well as advice on community services. There are now over 1,000 American FISH chapters.* While many tributes have been paid to the volunteer worker, few people cite good neighborliness. Yet in an urban society like ours, all too often a "disordered list of individuals," it is the informal, unorganized actions of the good neighbor which can make satisfactory relationships possible.

Volunteering is a proven means of establishing oneself in a community. The following letter to the editor expresses the sentiment well:

> *Through your "Opportunities for Volunteers" column, I, as a newcomer to town, found a way to integrate myself into the community, and expend my energies and abilities into channels I enjoy. The work is useful and I feel my services are needed.*

The writer goes on to report that she volunteers her services as public relations expert, assisting with publications for voluntary organizations.

Further, studies indicate that "as the length of residence increases, participation in community organizations also increases. Residents who participate in community organizations are more satisfied with their community than those who don't."**

The Newcomer with a Marketable Skill

Anyone with a marketable skill can use it to find a footing in a new region. Laurie was a teacher of English as a second language for many years. When her family was

---

*For further information, contact: FISH International, 18 Main Street, Lenox, Massachusetts 01240.

**James W. Matthews and John F. Thompson, "When People Move . . . ," in *Journal of Extension*, vol. X, no. 2, Summer 1972, pp. 29-35.

forced to move to Florida recently, she was quite upset; she loved her community and hated to leave her friends behind. She doubted that she could ever feel at home in such a totally different environment.

A recent letter shows how she used her skill to make new friends and how volunteering was crucial in her adaptation to new surroundings:

> *When we first arrived here, I didn't know a soul. You know that it takes me a while to make friends, and I felt desperately alone. Finally, I decided to go out and do something . . . . And sure enough, that was the turning point . . . . I went back to the University here for a one-year advanced degree in education, and now instead of teaching English to foreigners myself, I am teaching others how to teach English to Cuban refugees. I am now a teacher of teachers! . . . While I hesitated to take this volunteer job, having had the usual misgivings about volunteering, it provides an excellent opportunity to meet the kind of people I really like, and now I feel very much at home here.*

Political work can be a great social equalizer. Political volunteer work opens a whole new world of meeting people of all backgrounds, especially for the newcomer to town.

The Newcomer as a Volunteer in Politics

Alice arrived in Massachusetts three years ago. Her own account shows how important volunteer work was for her:

> *Julia Kerry and I were both newcomers to the state. We found that we shared many interests, and a close friendship developed between us. Julia's husband, John Kerry, original founder of the Vietnam Veterans Against the War, decided to run for Congress in 1972. I was in on the planning and strategy sessions and was asked what role I would like to play in the campaign. Because I knew that*

my commitment had to be limited due to family considerations (two children, aged eight and ten), I volunteered to do fund-raising. This way I could set time limits, and do some work at home on my own schedule, or so I thought! In retrospect, it was a hectic time with a lot of detailed work.

The personal satisfaction of working for a candidate in whom I believed deeply was great. Getting to know many different people among the electorate who shared the same principles and aspirations more than compensated me for the absence of pay and time spent away from home.

I discovered as a volunteer worker during the campaign that my family found my outside activities as stimulating as I did and enjoyed sharing my anecdotes and tales of woe. It seemed to bring an added dimension to our family life to have a mother as well as a father out and active in the world. Now I am accepting a part-time paid job as an administrator.

Newcomers like Alice, willing to play an active role in local affairs, may quickly become leaders in the community even though they are recent arrivals on the scene.

It is generally acknowledged that relocation of one's home, even under the most favorable circumstances, entails a series of difficult psychological adjustments. Noninvolvement or, at best, limited participation in community affairs, has been sharply criticized by those who see in it a menace to the traditional ideal of grass-roots democracy. Voluntarism is one proven means to counteract the "loss of commitment" that futurologists have noted among the "high mobiles." Aside from allowing newcomers to reaffirm their commitment, volunteer service also places them in contact with the members of their new community and provides an excellent opportunity to make friends.

PART THREE

Practical Resources

16

How to Locate a Suitable Volunteer Job

It is just as important to get good counsel and guidance in trying to find suitable and satisfactory volunteer work as it is in seeking paid employment. If you are at all bewildered by the seemingly endless list of ways in which you could use your talents in a volunteer position, you can save many hours of frustrating search by consulting one of the volunteer placement services which exist in cities and in many smaller communities throughout the country. There are two national directories of Voluntary Action Centers and Volunteer Bureaus listing approximately 300 such offices.* Canada presently boasts some 35 volunteer bureaus of its own.

Since I happen to be living and working in Boston, I shall use my personal knowledge of the resources in this city to give an idea of what is available in one city and what services to look for in other towns. I know their equivalents are available elsewhere, certainly in the cities but also to some

*One directory is published by the United Way of America, Voluntarism Division, 801 North Fairfax Street, Alexandria, Virginia 22314, and includes offices in Canada and Mexico in addition to the United States; and the other, a Directory of Voluntary Action Centers and Volunteer Bureaus, is put out by the National Center for Voluntary Action, 1785 Massachusetts Avenue, N.W., Washington, D.C. 20036.

extent in rural areas. In the latter communities, local church groups, granges, town meetings, United Funds, chapters of national organizations such as the Y, the 4-H Club, the Red Cross, etc., often function as the catalyst, the focal point for citizen participation. And even the newer self-help groups, the organizations for social change, the hotlines, etc., are to be found in unsuspected and out-of-the way places. *Work Force*, published by Vocations for Social Change, 4911 Telegraph Avenue, Oakland, California 94609, lists many such groups. The work of WOW (Wider Opportunities for Women), which was started by volunteers in Washington, D.C., has now spread to include branches not only in Boston (C. F. Hurley Building, Government Center, Boston 02114) but also in smaller communities such as White River Junction, Vermont.

If needed volunteer placement services do not exist, it is quite feasible to start your own, and you can readily draw on the experience of others. The National Center for Voluntary Action at 1785 Massachusetts Avenue, N.W., Washington, D.C. 20036, maintains a Clearinghouse to help with such endeavors. Their information service is valuable, extensive, and prompt. You do not need to declare your party affiliation to use it! Nor do you need to agree with official government policy to benefit from its factual information on the mechanics of starting and running a volunteer placement service.

As for Boston, the two major most knowledgeable volunteer placement agencies in the area are:

> The Voluntary Action Center of Metropolitan
>   Boston
> 14 Somerset Street,
> Boston, Massachusetts 02108
> Phone: 742-2000

> The Civic Center and Clearing House, Inc.
> 14 Beacon Street,
> Boston, Massachusetts 02108
> Phone: 227-1762

They cooperate closely with one another and freely exchange information and refer clients to each other.

The *Voluntary Action Center* (known as VAC), which is a part of the United Community Planning Corporation, is the Boston affiliate of the National Center for Voluntary Action. It publishes an extensive list of well over 300 volunteer openings every spring and fall and makes telephone referrals, as well as placements after personal interviews. It is equipped to handle groups of people anxious to work on a joint project and keeps a current inventory of suitable group projects. The VAC acts as consultant to United Way and other agencies and assists them in finding volunteer help throughout the year and for single occasions or emergencies.

The *Civic Center and Clearing House, Inc.*, is an independent nonprofit organization which keeps constantly revised and updated files of volunteer opportunities throughout the metropolitan area. Seven years ago it initiated a weekly newspaper column, "Opportunities for Volunteers," in the *Boston Globe*, which it continues to coordinate.* The particular emphasis of the Civic Center and Clearing House is on individual counseling, placement, and follow-up. It is primarily interested in helping those persons anxious to volunteer for an extended period of time. Its unique wrinkle is supplied by its affiliated Career and Vocational Advisory Service, which is particularly helpful to many would-be volunteers.**

To meet the demand by working men and women anxious to give service—and that demand is steadily increasing—the *Hello Pages*, 14 pages listing evening and weekend openings for

*"Opportunities for Volunteers" appears every Wednesday in the "Living" section. The press, TV, and radio are other good sources to locate volunteer openings. Newspapers elsewhere provide similar public service by listing "want ads" for volunteers (free of charge).

**Also affiliated with the Civic Center and Clearing House is the Adult and Student Placement Service of the Parents League of Greater Boston.

volunteers, were prepared jointly by the Civic Center and Clearing House and the Voluntary Action Center.*

The *City of Boston* had its own *Volunteer Coordinating Program (City Corps)* at City Hall, funded under a one-year federal grant. Forty similar grants to cities, counties, or regional governments were made by ACTION on a one-year basis only. Therefore the future of these programs is uncertain.

In this student-oriented town, many schools and universities maintain their own volunteer placement services, and students are well advised to consult these first.

Senior citizens (60 and over) may wish to join RSVP (Retired Senior Volunteer Program), which has sixteen regional clearinghouses throughout Massachusetts alone. The current state liaison office is located at

> The Executive Office of Elder Affairs, RSVP
> 120 Boylston Street,
> Boston, Massachusetts 02116

Three regional offices can be found at

> Boston RSVP
> 1 City Hall Square
> Boston, Massachusetts 02201

> Eastern Middlesex County RSVP
> Post Office Box A
> Somerville, Massachusetts 02145
> (covering 11 communities)

> Newton, Wellesley, Weston RSVP
> 429 Cherry Street
> West Newton, Massachusetts 02165

This is a national program which operates throughout the country and functions in slightly different styles depending

---

*The *Hello Pages* may be ordered from the Civic Center and Clearing House, Inc., 14 Beacon Street, Boston, Massachusetts 02108, for $1, postpaid.

upon the region. Training specifically designed for senior citizens who wish to work as information specialists with other senior citizens is provided under a Title III federal grant, by the

> Massachusetts Association
> of Older Americans
> 110 Arlington Street
> Boston, Massachusetts 02116

Serving as a volunteer clearinghouse for ten towns west of Boston in the Nashoba Valley is

> Widening Horizons, Inc.
> 115 Stow Street
> Concord, Massachusetts 01742

Among the most experienced and largest volunteer programs in the city are the

> School Volunteers for Boston
> 16 Arlington Street
> Boston, Massachusetts 02116
> and the

> School Volunteer Project—Cambridge
> 1700 Cambridge Street
> Cambridge, Massachusetts 02138

Between them they place many thousands of volunteers in the public school system. They do their own recruiting, interviewing, screening, and training of volunteers. School Volunteer programs exist now and continue to spring up in many local school systems. There is a national affiliation of Public School Volunteers, the National School Volunteer Program, 450 North Grand Avenue, Los Angeles, California 90012.

And, last but not least, check with the volunteer director of your local hospital or any hospital of your choice. Placements vary a great deal. Make your interests clear, be imaginative, and do not have yourself assigned to the accident ward if you are really more interested in doing laboratory work. If you are not qualified or need to refresh your skills, you may be taken on as a volunteer trainee, labor-union rules permitting.

Many of the sources listed in Appendix A may also be consulted when in search of a volunteer position. *Call for Action*, wherever it is in operation, can make the necessary referrals.

A report was issued for the Commonwealth of Massachusetts in December 1973 by the Governor's Commission on Citizen Participation, which came up with far-reaching recommendations for stepped-up active volunteer involvement by the public in governmental agencies.

Eventually, intensive recruitment of volunteers through the public media may require computers to match large numbers of volunteers with volunteer openings.

Talent Pools

Talent pools constitute a special kind of clearinghouse for volunteers. Whereas most volunteer counseling and placement services work with applicants as they turn up seeking placement, the talent pool clearinghouse actually keeps an inventory of volunteers who have specific talents to contribute. As needs arise and requests are received for volunteers with specialized skills, the talent pool staff can make referrals from among its registered clientele.

In 1960, members of a senior center outside Chicago sparked the idea of such a pool. For the most part, they were retired business executives and professionals who felt that their experience ought to be put to continued use. As a first step they contacted nearby schools, offering to lecture to classes and conduct foreign language seminars. Some of the schools accepted.

Three years later, the Winnetka Talent Pool, a nonprofit

organization staffed entirely by volunteers, was working with hundreds of men and women aged 18 to 87. Though it is true that schools all over the country were beginning to work with volunteers, this particular talent pool in Winnetka set the stage for the nationwide acceptance of Volunteer School Aides.

Since its inception, this talent pool has branched out into many of the types of volunteer activities described throughout this book. In addition, they have published *An Operating Manual for a Volunteer Talent Pool.* *

In the introduction to this excellent manual we read:

> *For many decades, individuals have given service to agencies and organizations of all kinds: schools, libraries, welfare agencies, hospitals, etc. . . . Today volunteering carries, in addition to a new sense of responsibility, a growing conviction that each person should be a contributing member of the community.*

The contents of this manual are as pertinent today as at the time of publication.

In Fort Vancouver you can check "volunteer people" out at the Regional Library — volunteers who are willing to teach nuclear physics, home canning, fly fishing, or crewel embroidery! The People Index** lists some 150 different skills,*** is kept up to date, and is not limited to academic areas. The

---

An Operating Manual for a Volunteer Talent Pool, edited by Janet Burgoon and Joan Winter (Winnetka, Illinois: Volunteer Talent Pool, 1967). Available from publisher, at 739 Elm Street, Winnetka, Illinois 60093. Recommended reading.

**For further information write: The People Index, Fort Vancouver Regional Library, 1007 East Mill Plain Boulevard, Vancouver, Washington 98663.

***Classification of skills was based on the Dewey Decimal System used in libraries and could be adapted to any talent pool or skills bank operation. See a detailed description in *An Operating Manual for a Volunteer Talent Pool,* pages 25-27.

indexers have taken care to prevent the file's becoming a commercial directory. All persons listed offer their knowledge and services for free. Close cooperation between the library and the local volunteer bureau guarantees continuous volunteer jobs for anyone desiring more than a casual involvement.

Emergencies often arise which call for the immediate services of an interpreter. A badly burned Pakistani seaman was rushed to a Seattle hospital. He spoke no English, was terrified by the strange surroundings, and no one understood him. He resisted all treatment and eventually died. This incident inspired the creation of the Seattle Language Bank.

This specialized talent pool now includes some 350 volunteer interpreters in 80 languages and dialects. At first, volunteers were recruited from the University of Washington. Word spread, and many Seattle citizens began to volunteer. It is they who are the stable force, since students are not usually permanent residents. Volunteers can be contacted through an around-the-clock medical telephone exchange service.

Since the tragedy which inspired the language bank, a volunteer has learned to explain the technique of operating a kidney machine in Portuguese; others have been interpreters at murder trials; and the bank has been able to supply multilingual baby sitters. Through this special talent pool Japanese residents learned of an aged Japanese man who was destitute and without family. They interpreted his Social Security benefits for him and continue to look after him.

This entire service represents an unusual combination of talent pool and hotline.

Two Sample Lists of Volunteer Categories

Before consulting one of the volunteer placement offices, you may want to glance through the following lists, which give some idea of the variety of volunteer categories and possible projects.

The first list was compiled for a national *1972/73 Directory of College Student Volunteer Programs,* published by ACTION, in Washington, D.C.

The second index was put out by the Clearing House of the National Center for Voluntary Action in Washington. Programs are grouped under major headings such as Civic Affairs, Education, Legal Rights, etc.

VOLUNTEER CATEGORIES

The following list was taken from the *1972/73 Directory of College Student Volunteer Programs.* Because of space limitations, volunteer projects have been broadly classified into sixteen areas. It is helpful to read through the wide range of projects that a particular area encompasses.

Community Service
Clearinghouse
Fundraising
One-time community
  drives
Hotline
Emergency action
Community publications
Community research/
  surveys
Community planning
Housing improvement
Architect/engineer
  services
Income tax assistance
Business aid

Civic Affairs
Voter registration
Canvassing
Lobbying
Petitioning
Proposing legislation

Drugs
Youth education
Community education
Counseling
Hotline
Walk-in center
Halfway house
Emergency assistance

Recreation
   Sports
   Arts & crafts
   Field trips
   Drama
   Dance
   Summer camps
   Special projects

Education
   Educational counseling
   Preschool
   School-age tutoring
   Teacher Aides
   Adult education
   Alternative schools

Health
   Nutritional education
   Breakfast program
   Health education
   Sex education
   Hospital visitation
   General hospital services
   Clinics
   Dental services
   Family planning
   Abortion referral

Legal Assistance
   Draft information
   Welfare rights
   Tenants rights
   Investigative research
   Storefront
   Public defender

Ecology
   Youth education
   Community education
   Clean-ups
   Recycling
   Research
   Political action
   Conservation

Consumer Services
   Consumer education
   Consumer complaints
   Consumer protection
   Investigations/surveys
   Financial management
   Cooperatives
   Credit unions

Religious Activity
   Religious education
   Visitation
   Bible study

Corrections
In the Institution:
   Counseling/legal aid
   Education
   Job skills
   Recreation
   Companionship
   Employer recruitment

Out of the Institution:
   Court/parole/or probation
      assistance
   Halfway house

Reintegration into com-
munity
Employer recruitment

Aging
Meals-on-wheels
Companionship
Letter writing
Social activities
Visitation
Transportation
Political activity

Youth-Oriented Services
Big brother
Big sister
Teen centers
Coffee houses
Rap sessions

Campus Related Activities
Peer tutoring
Cooperatives
Hotline
Ombudsman
Fund-raising
Handicapped assistance
Draft counseling
Legal assistance

Handicapped
Halfway house
Tutoring
Recreation
Basic skills
Therapy
Counseling
Transportation

NATIONAL CENTER FOR VOLUNTARY ACTION, WASHINGTON, D.C., CLEARINGHOUSE INDEX

Civic Affairs
Stimulating citizen interest in government, assisting in voter registration, proposing legislation, lobbying . . .

Communications and Public Relations
Writing newsletters; preparing brochures/bulletins/ educational material; developing information for TV/ radio/newspaper releases; forming speakers bureaus . . .

Community Service
Reaching out to find people in need; organizing self-help groups; developing information and referral centers; involving youth in community projects; forming coalitions for

planning and action; assessing community needs; serving on advisory bodies to government . . .

Consumer Services

Providing financial and budget counseling; educating consumers who may be particularly vulnerable to shady credit and installment deals; handling consumer complaints through "action line" telephone services; forming buying groups and cooperatives; conducting legislative research in areas of consumer concern; investigating fraud . . .

Cultural Activities

Teaching art; adding music programs to schools; providing theater; developing general enrichment opportunities; conducting museum tours; sponsoring art centers . . .

Education

Serving as teacher aides; tutoring students from kindergarten through high school; working with adult illiterates; helping dropouts to resume studies; teaching English as a second language; building up library services; holding story hours; raising money for those who are college material but can't afford higher education; contributing skills and expertise to a school talent bank; setting up preschools . . .

Employment and Jobs

Counseling young people on career planning; mounting career fairs; working on equal opportunity employment drives; upgrading skills; finding summer jobs; providing placement services . . .

Entrepreneurship

Giving technical and/or financial advice to struggling businesses; providing management training; assisting minority businessmen . . .

Family, Youth, and Children-Oriented Services

Providing day-care services; involving parents in their

children's development; adopting a welfare family; sharing housekeeping abilities; working on grooming and social skills . . .

Give-away programs
Providing emergency food/clothes/household equipment; running holiday gift bureaus; operating thrift shops . . .

Health and Mental Health
Working in hospitals and clinics; assisting in the therapeutic process with the emotionally ill/alcoholic/drug-addicted; educating young and old on the prevention of disease; helping in family-planning efforts; operating hotlines; contributing to rehabilitation programs; reintegrating patients back into community life . . .

Housing
Improving existing structures in rundown areas; developing nonprofit programs to build new houses; investigating offenses against fair-housing laws; facilitating tenant-landlord relationships . . .

Interracial/Interethnic/Intergroup Relations
Conducting workshops/conferences to improve interracial relations; forming coalitions among religious denominations to tackle common problems; participating in efforts for integration; establishing programs to reach inner-city people; setting up interracial home-visiting programs; bridging the generation gap . . .

Legal Rights, Law Enforcement, and Crime Prevention
Assisting in probation/parole programs; working with juveniles to prevent delinquency; providing legal services; relating to prisoners; helping former prisoners return to the community; improving police-community relations; establishing volunteer programs in juvenile institutions; court watching . . .

Nutrition

Teaching food selection and preparation; developing school lunch programs; helping in school cafeterias; aiding in food distribution; delivering meals to the old/ill/handicapped . . .

Organization and Administration in Volunteerism

Operating volunteer centers; recruiting volunteers; giving awards; compiling directories of volunteer opportunities . . .

Physical Environment

Fighting the further spread of pollution through research/data gathering/code enforcement; restoring land and waters; contributing to conservation education; creating playgrounds and parks; cleaning up litter; getting rid of rats; working for population control; abating noise; operating recycling centers . . .

Psychological/Social Support Services

Filling the role of big brother or big sister in the lives of children in need of additional adult relationships; providing companionship to the shut-in; aiding unwed mothers; developing halfway-house programs; telephone counseling; assisting in nursing homes . . .

Recreation

Providing play activities and play space; coaching sports; teaching arts and crafts; giving parties for children/senior citizens; developing vacation programs; establishing drop-in centers/club facilities . . .

Transportation

Chauffeuring the aged/the ill/the handicapped/the poor; taking part in driver education and other safety programs; upgrading community transportation . . .

17

Take-Charge Volunteer Projects

For certain people, volunteering offers more than the opportunity to work for an organization; some perceive needs and problems by themselves and tackle them individually. These people create their own volunteer jobs, in a sense, acting as one-person volunteer organizations. Sometimes their initiative inspires others, and these entrepreneurs may find themselves spearheading an entire movement. At other times, their focus is narrower, and once a project has been completed, they move on to something else. In any case, these take-charge persons all have one thing in common: they like to get things done and have the motivation and perseverance to take on a challenge and stay with it. The stories of these volunteers, the ones who choose to "write their own tickets," are as diverse as the concerns of our society.

Wheeling Through Boston and the Blue Line: A Walking Tour of Boston

The handicapped or physically disabled are citizens whose needs are easily overlooked.* While many volunteers work with the handicapped in institutions, one woman chose to put her energies into a take-charge project for

*See Chapter 18, "Hotlines and Self-Help Project," p. 188, for a description of what the physically disabled are doing for themselves.

those who are confined to wheelchairs but otherwise able to get around. Appalled by the many architectural barriers encountered by the physically disabled, and inspired by a guidebook, *London for the Handicapped,* she made it her business to survey the city of Boston for accessibility by wheelchair.

She planned the guide, recruited and organized volunteers to help her, and personally investigated hundreds of buildings, checking stairways and ramps, door widths, restrooms, theater aisles, etc. She received backing for this publication from the Easter Seal Society, and the resulting pamphlet, *Wheeling Through Boston,** is now available free of charge. Others have seen her example and are already at work on similar booklets.**

A survey of a different nature was undertaken by an enterprising volunteer with a special interest in history and writing. Attracted by a notice in the "Opportunities for Volunteers" listing in the *Boston Globe,* this volunteer picked up the idea of laying out an alternative route to the overused "Freedom Trail." Single-handedly Mary researched and wrote *The Blue Line: A Walking Tour of Boston.*† The design and printing of the pamphlet was made possible by voluntary contributions. The *Tour* is now distributed by the tourist information booth located in the State House, staffed entirely by volunteers.

Consumer Groups

The example of Ralph Nader, nationally known consumer advocate, has inspired individual citizens to

---

*Wheeling Through Boston, prepared by Paula Lutzin and printed as a public service by the Easter Seal Society for Crippled Children and Adults of Massachusetts, Inc.

**The Wheelchair Traveler, by Douglas R. Armand, Bale Hill Road, Milford, New Hampshire.

† The Blue Line: A Walking Tour of Boston — Beacon Hill to Back Bay, prepared by Mary VanMeter for the Civic Center and Clearing House, Inc., 14 Beacon Street, Boston, Massachusetts. Copies available at 50 cents each, postpaid.

form volunteer consumer groups throughout the nation. A special presidential assistant on consumer affairs says of these volunteer-initiated projects,

> *they provide valuable services to the individual consumers, helping them to resolve their complaints and educating them to be more effective shoppers.*

While the methods of establishing consumer protection groups vary, a New York organizer's description of her group is typical:

1. *People had nowhere to turn, so we decided to form our own group. As a result of personal experiences involving dissatisfaction with products and lack of attention by business, a group of five of us got together informally.*
2. *We limited our number to avoid the problems of bureaucracy. Convinced that we had to act, we organized ourselves: one of us handles incoming calls, another documents complaints, a third mediates between buyers and sellers, while the remaining two serve as secretary and treasurer, respectively.*
3. *We handle complaints on a wide range of consumer interests and hold meetings to educate the public and allow them to let off steam. We lobby as a group for better consumer legislation. Our services are free to all members of the community as long as they agree to support consumer legislation.* *

Clean Up Children's TV

As a result of complaints about excessive violence and nonstop commercials on children's television programs, four determined and energetic mothers** have taken on the TV industry. That is how ACT (Action for Children's Television) was born. From all over the country they received comments such as this:

Child: I love the TV—it is my friend.
Mother: It is sad that my child's "friend" betrays him and shows him things that make him afraid to sleep at night.

ACT, which has grown into a sizable group of parents and professionals, is fighting "to end the commercial exploitation of children on children's television" by:

1. *Co-sponsoring a national questionnaire on children's television*

---

*Adapted from a statement by Myra Wilson, founder and organizer of LICPU (the Long Island Consumer Protection Union).

**Evelyn Sarson, Lillian Ambrosino, Judith Chalfen, Peggy Charrer. National Headquarters: ACT, 46 Austin Street, Newtonville, Massachusetts 02160.

habits and analyzing the returns, which already number more than 25,000;

2. *Filing complaints with the FTC (Federal Trade Commission) against major advertisers and several television networks;*

3. *Testifying before the Senate Select Committee on Nutrition and Human Needs, which is studying the effects of children's TV advertising. (ACT is disturbed that "advertising for children is dominated by sugary products, endangering the health of future generations.")*

Whether they expected it or not, these four women ended up spearheading a national movement which has now spread abroad. Eighty representatives of broadcasting groups from around the world recently attended an international seminar in Munich, Germany, to discuss ideas and information regarding children's TV.

Litter

Trash is an insult to something naturally attractive, a sign that people feel separated from their environment. Litter on our streets is a constant eyesore and a reminder of people's carelessness. This is the kind of problem where take-charge volunteers *can* make a difference. While one individual's efforts may not change the situation in an entire city, the woman wearing work gloves and carrying plastic disposal bags who was recently observed picking up trash along the riverbank makes other people aware of the problem and prods them into lending a hand.

Even though a national trash picker-uppers' organization is unlikely to emerge and volunteer trash collectors will continue to go unheralded, this type of activity does represent yet another aspect of volunteer initiative.

Trees in the City

While walking past row after row of apartment houses on the streets of a European city one hot afternoon, Doreen felt a vague sense of oppression. Suddenly she realized that there were no trees to be seen. This realization so startled her that she determined to look into the distribution of shade trees in her native city on her return home.

Her memory had not tricked her. In Boston she found many more sidewalk trees, even in less affluent neighborhoods. But further investigation led to the discovery that many of these trees were in poor condition. Some were dying. General neglect, lack of professional attention, air pollution, and the Dutch elm disease were all taking their toll.

Up until this time, horticulture had not been one of Doreen's major interests. But she decided to learn all she could about trees, especially their adaptability to city environments. She managed to arouse her husband's interest in the project. When he and a few of their friends announced that they were willing to study along with her, they turned to the Horticultural Society and the Arnold Arboretum for help. The librarians there became so impressed with these enthusiastic and persistent students that they offered their personal assistance.

As a first step, a citywide survey of shade trees was mapped out. Doreen and her volunteer friends were trained by the staff of the Arboretum. These professionals conducted tours of various areas and taught the volunteers to identify different kinds of trees. They also showed them how to detect early signs of disease.

Eventually, the volunteers submitted a report of the shade tree survey to City Hall. As a result of their recommendations, and much to the credit of a few municipal employees, action was taken: new planting of young trees is under way.

Another consequence of this individual volunteer organizer's effort is the formation of a regular volunteer program at the Arnold Arboretum — one of the few volunteer associations I have encountered who do not need to "beat the bushes" for new members . . .

Sailmaker

Special skills and a little imagination sometimes lend themselves to unusual volunteer enterprises. Take the New England sailmaker who organizes and instructs a group of boating enthusiasts in the design and manufacture of sails. Boston's Community Boating, Inc., which maintains a large fleet of sailboats, puts them to good use, permitting city residents to enjoy the luxury of sailing on the Charles River at minimal cost. At once-a-week winter work sessions the volunteer group mends and replaces sails, thereby making more boats available for summer recreation.

Living History Project

Julia is the originator of the "Living History Project," a study of Hitler's victims now living in the United

States. She and others like her recognized the urgency of recording *oral* history of the Hitler period before this testimony became lost forever. Originally conceived of by a few women, this volunteer project has assumed national proportions; hundreds of volunteers will work an estimated five years to complete it.

Inspired by the Hebrew University's oral history study recording the experiences of those Israelis who lived through the holocaust, Julia and her colleagues decided to apply the same technique here. "We hope to make it possible for historians of the future to hear through tapes the recollections of the nearly half-million Hitler victims now living in the United States." While numerous books and articles have been written about the better-known figures among this group of emigrants, there is little documentation on how the average refugee managed to live after leaving Europe. The "Living History Project" seeks to fill this gap by recording the experiences of some of the hundreds of thousands who had to flee. Such a study will be invaluable to scholars, writers, and journalists, university departments of sociology, psychology, and history, as well as to Jewish organizations of all kinds.

The technique of oral history, fast becoming an important part of twentieth-century documentation, is particularly appropriate for this task. Trained volunteers contact former refugees from Nazi oppression and ask permission to meet with them in their homes. Armed with a carefully prepared questionnaire designed to stimulate autobiographical reflection, as well as tape recorders, these volunteers spend many hours with each subject. Following the interview, the recorded text is transcribed and submitted to the person interviewed to be read, and, if necessary, corrected. It is then initialed as being authentic, making it a historical document. Volunteers catalog the tapes, which are later made available for evaluation.

The "Living History Project" has been adopted by the

Brandeis University National Women's Committee. Specifically citing the availability of volunteer work power for the undertaking of a project of such dimension, the committee chairperson, Julia Thurman, said:

> *. . . here are volunteers with the interest, the time, the ability, and the dedication to seek out the survivors and tape interviews with them.*

Thus a volunteer network has sprung up around the country, including coordinators, staff, interviewers, and interviewees. It is truly a volunteer organization from start to finish.

The Story of Louise Bruyn: A Unique "Take-Charge" Project

Louise was an ordinary suburban housewife and mother of three teenagers until on February 17, 1971, she obeyed the demands of her conscience, setting out on a 450-mile walk from Boston to Washington, D.C. Conceived as a protest against the war in Vietnam, the walk took 45 days. The many people who followed her daily progress in the press were with her in spirit, but Louise walked alone.

In terms of this book, Louise Bruyn might be considered an anomaly. Her work for peace in Indochina is in the nature of a "calling." It is neither a return to any previous career nor a typical volunteer activity, for it lacks intentional timing and structure. The walk was something that happened—something that had to be done — not something to be dovetailed with family activities at a specific time, but a burden that, at one particular moment in history, had to be assumed.

As Quakers, she and her family had been very much aware of the war in Southeast Asia for years. Through Friends Meetings the family's interest in nonviolence and the Peace Movement grew. From this philosophical awareness Louise moved to action: first, a series of peace marches, and then extensive work in the McCarthy presidential campaign. The

decision to make the trek to Washington—the trek that made
her a public figure—came in a flash as she was reading an
article describing how the American people appeared to be
anesthetized and unable to make a move to end the war.
Instantly the idea of a walk from her home to Washington
materialized. It would be witness to what one individual could
do.

Though her previous activities for peace could be considered "volunteer" work, from this point on her crusade
became an almost mystical experience. Louise talks quietly
about the love she first felt, the support she got from friends
and family, how the ripples from one little pebble had far-
reaching effects. People came to her house to man a 24-hour
switchboard and to bring food for her family. Other people
discovered that they too could do something. Louise's
determination and initiative gave them the motivation to
mobilize themselves and others — a sort of chain reaction
was set off.

What kind of woman would have the courage and physical
stamina for such an undertaking?

Louise Bruyn would be the first to insist that there is
nothing extraordinary about her. She grew up in Chicago, one
of four children in a close-knit family. Her mother, a concert
pianist, was a very able woman. Everybody in the family
helped out around the house; Louise learned early to do
things for herself.

At college, she became involved with theater and dance.
She kept extremely busy and thrived on it. She had no time
for volunteer work then. Louise was an elementary schoolteacher until her first child was born. She then taught dance
two days a week, organizing her own groups, and she
participated in the local community theater, eventually
becoming its president. While her three children were small,
she felt that all of these outside activities had become "too
much," and she gave them up. Her life was largely family-

directed. Where outside interests were concerned, they were carefully related to the family schedule, and she discarded them when they seemed to infringe.

Louise Bruyn was not really involved in any volunteer activity until she took part in the planning for the first peace moratorium in 1966. She volunteered to become secretary of the group and in a month became the coordinator. Then followed peace marches and campaign work, until, at the time of the invasion of Cambodia, she made her famous march on Washington.

Louise's crusade did not end with the march. She then became involved with a group of women who want to go to North Vietnam to help rebuild that war-torn country. As "Women Volunteers to Vietnam," they hope to live at peasant level with no special protection or privileges.

One feels that Louise will not be content with the achievement of a nominal peace, and that as long as anything more can be done for war-scarred Vietnam, she will want to do it. Already under way is an organized effort to facilitate the adoption of Vietnamese war orphans by American families. And for the present, American women here can work to support orphanages, refugee camps, and self-help economic programs in Vietnam.

Louise is constantly looking for ways to sustain the energy that was mobilized at the time of her walk.

18

Hotlines and Self-Help Projects

During the Cuban missile crisis, President Kennedy used the Hotline to communicate instantly with Premier Khrushchev. At that critical moment it was important that these two world leaders could pick up the phone to prevent trouble based on the lack of information or a misunderstanding.

The idea of crisis-intervention "hotlines" has been adopted by ordinary citizens, particularly the young, in most urban centers throughout the country. It is a new way of reaching people, where traditional channels have failed. People in trouble can call a local hotline and immediately find someone at the other end to talk to, someone who can meet them on their own level without making moral judgments. The problems of the callers vary:

They may be connected with the use of drugs or alcohol.

Lonely and depressed people wish to talk about their worries with another human being, to hear a human voice.

The sexual revolution is creating new problems, while alleviating existing ones, for young and old, females and males. Community sex information hotlines give counseling over the phone on topics ranging from VD to pregnancies, including all aspects of birth control, family planning, and abortion, or give support and advice to pregnant women alone who wish to carry their babies to term.

Volunteer organizations set up to help the troubled or the sick have existed for a long time. Hotlines are one logical up-to-date extension of such social services. While hotlines may come and go in response to changing problems, the anonymity they provide, the distant, nonthreatening way to get instant support, instant service, have given people a new channel to help. If more than a telephone conversation is necessary, good hotline volunteers can put the caller in touch with appropriate agencies.

Suicide prevention hotlines are among the best known, both in this country and abroad. Often a person in misery and despair just needs someone to talk to. Volunteers have taken the initiative in establishing and manning around-the-clock phone lines to try to help those human beings desperate enough to consider taking their own lives. One such group, "The Samaritans," started in England in 1953. By now some 150 local offices exist there, with branches in Rhodesia, India, and New Zealand. Their newsletter reports on their volunteers:

> *The 12,000 trained Samaritans in Great Britain are from every kind of background; but business men, teachers, clerical workers, housewives and retired men and women are the most noticeable in numbers . . . some Samaritans are as young as eighteen.*

The Samaritans have started branch offices in the United States. They afford a splendid example of a volunteer organization which insists on a rigorous selection process and thorough preparation of its volunteer workers:

> *The training of these volunteers is all-important. Both clergy and lay people learn skills together, varying from careful record-keeping to expert use of the telephone . . . to understanding how*

not *to play at amateur psychiatry . . . . A variety of training methods is used, including discussion and tutorial groups, as well as role playing. The telephone volunteers are backed up by a trained professional staff.*

One hotline designed with a rather special clientele in mind exists in Washington, D.C. It may sound paradoxical, but this telephone hotline is for the deaf. Hundreds of Washington area homes of deaf persons are connected through an elaborate telephone-teletype system, which prints out phone messages electronically. Volunteers working at the hotline office can thus communicate with some of our most isolated citizens. In case of emergency the volunteers can draw on a variety of professional people who know how to use sign language to communicate with the deaf.

Project Place, which was founded in Boston in 1967, is a good example of the fast-growing hotline industry. From the original hotline, set up specifically for drug counseling, information, and referral, it has greatly expanded so that Project Place is operating five action programs for drug-abuse prevention. Particularly interesting in connection with the overall development of a network of hotlines is its Project Reach. This is a service which has trained volunteers for more than two dozen other hotlines in the Greater Boston area. This service represents a serious attempt to reduce potentially harmful efforts by well-meaning but amateurish volunteers and helps suburban communities attempt to work out their own problems. While age and sex need not make a difference in the choice of hotline volunteers, some of the youth-directed hotlines definitely prefer young counselors, who have experienced some of the particular problems firsthand.

Aside from counseling by phone, people who share a common problem often do band together in concrete self-help projects. One of the best known of these is Alcoholics

Anonymous, recovered alcoholics trying to help those still suffering to dry out and make the difficult readjustment to society. The success of this well-established project is generally recognized.

Experience indicates that people with specific problems are more willing to accept help from volunteers who have themselves successfully overcome similar difficulties. The increasing number of halfway houses, whether they be for former drug addicts, recently released or paroled prisoners, or mental health patients immediately upon discharge from an institution, constitutes a more formalized attempt to let people help each other.

Project Volunteer Power, initiated by the handicapped, is one such self-help program. These people, now estimated at some 26.6 million in the United States, prefer to think of themselves as physically limited or rehabilitated, rather than "handicapped." Three pilot projects of PVP in Alabama, Massachusetts, and Minnesota aim at "bringing the handicapped into the mainstream of life, thus giving them an independence of spirit and eventually a self-supporting status." PVP has conducted citywide surveys of the handicapped as part of normal census taking. In this way, volunteers hope to identify the handicapped and their needs and to acquaint them with available services.

The American Cancer Society has integrated into its service programs "Reach to Recovery," a self-help organization composed of women who have undergone mastectomies (surgery for breast cancer). "Reach to Recovery" was founded by a woman who herself had such an operation and felt a severe lack of understanding help during and after this traumatic experience.

Volunteers, as well as the professionals involved, prepare patients to deal with the practical and emotional difficulties of this operation. Subsequently they assist these women in coming to terms with their condition. "Reach to Recovery" volunteers are all former mastectomy patients. They receive intensive training, first accompanying experienced volunteers before they may pay visits alone. Such visits go beyond mere assurances, and include practical advice on prostheses, exercises, clothing, and shopping hints. Most importantly, the volunteer talks to the patient; by her example she demonstrates that she herself has learned to live comfortably after the operation.

Still another group of females with a common problem has banded together to draw mutual support and counsel: women who have been raped. To serve the immediate and continuing needs of these women, a 24-hour emergency telephone service is available at Area Rape Crisis Centers. Staffed by women volunteers, these centers offer continued counseling and discussion groups, as well as medical, legal, and support services.

Yet, a self-help project need not concern itself with quite so dramatic a problem. For example, the increasing number of day-care centers that are springing up across the country are often organized by women who want to free themselves from the responsibilities of continuous child care (see Part Two, Chapter 10, "The Mother of Young Children").

The Sojourner Truth Day-Care Center in Chicago was organized by women with this common objective. Speaking about the center, one of the organizers said:

> *We got together as women, as sisters, and we did it. It's another proof that volunteer work doesn't have to be meaningless or patronizing. The whole thing is doing it for yourself, to cure your own social ills, to bring about social change that benefits your community.*

Appendix A: Counseling and Testing Services: Agencies Specializing in the Placement of Women

If you are planning to enter the working world, but are unsure about which direction to take, you would do well to consult a professional counseling and/or testing service. Fees run anywhere from $10 to $150, and the price charged does not necessarily reflect the quality of service rendered. You will find listings of such services for your area in the Yellow Pages of the telephone book under "Vocational and Educational Guidance" or the like.

A word of caution is in order here. Some of the commercial firms listed under such headings are simply employment agencies principally interested in the fees they can obtain. In dealing with employment agencies it is vitally important never to sign any contract without reading all of the fine print, and to avoid making any advance payments. If in doubt, it is advisable to consult the local Better Business Bureau. Some of the more respectable agencies get their fee from the employer instead of the applicant. At present, however, the demand for jobs is so much greater than the supply of openings that more and more agencies charge the job seeker.

Local universities sometimes offer counseling and testing services to the general public at a reasonable fee. The regional offices of both the YWCA and the YMCA often employ career and vocational guidance counselors.

A check of the women's counseling and resource centers in your town is recommended. Many of them are new, some are run as cooperatives, some are short-lived, and there may be a frequent turnover of staff. But if they are any good at all, these centers should have the kind of information you are looking for. Here, too, the YWCAs are making a special effort by opening their own women's resource and information centers. There are over five hundred NOW chapters, and they maintain reference libraries and job bulletin boards.

If you are a college graduate, the career and placement office of your alma mater should be among the first to be consulted. Write to your college even if you live in a different part of the country. Some of the college placement offices provide reciprocal services to alumnae of colleges elsewhere. If you are disappointed by the career counseling and placement help available through your school, work through local alumnae chapters to improve matters. Educational institutions are susceptible to alumnae pressure, particularly in today's world. Professional schools and associations should and often do help with job referrals.

Adult education centers frequently run career clinics and job preparation workshops as part of their continuing education programs. Local public schools sometimes provide such seminars or extension courses for adults. The public library in your town is likely to have a fund of information which should not be overlooked. In many cities the "underground" and the feminist press carry helpful hints and advertisements.

The *Women's Almanac*, a magazine published by the Armitage Press, Inc., 1430 Massachusetts Avenue, Cambridge, Massachusetts 02138, carries inserts and lists relevant to residents of:

Atlanta	Memphis
Baltimore	Milwaukee
Boston	Minneapolis/St. Paul
Chicago	New Orleans
Dallas	New York/Manhattan
Detroit	Philadelphia
Hartford	Pittsburgh
New Haven	Providence
Houston	St. Louis
Los Angeles/	San Francisco Bay Area
Southern California	Washington, D.C.

Copies can be ordered directly from the publisher.

The *Women's Yellow Pages*, the original source book for women, which first appeared in Boston in 1972 and again in 1974, will, I hope, be distributed nationally with local reference lists inserted. Direct inquiries to: Boston Women's Collective, Inc., 490 Beacon Street, Boston, Massachusetts 02115.

"Catalyst," headquartered in New York City, provides services to meet the needs of women at various stages of career development. Catalyst has compiled a comprehensive list of its national network of local resource centers, which (as of January 1974) can be found in the following states:

California	Missouri
Colorado	New Jersey
Connecticut	New York
Delaware	North Carolina
Florida	Ohio
Georgia	Oregon
Illinois	Pennsylvania
Indiana	Texas
Iowa	Virginia
Kansas	Washington
Massachusetts	Wisconsin
Michigan	Wyoming

Although there is only one listing for Colorado and for Minnesota so far, there are thirteen listings for California and nine for Pennsylvania. Catalyst's network is constantly expanding and is well monitored from the New York head office. The description of its affiliates is detailed and updated regularly. Catalyst is experimenting with a computerized national roster, which is open to women age 24 and over who have completed at least one year of college and who seek administrative, managerial, technical, or professional positions. Information on all of Catalyst's services and a copy of the National Network List are sent to all women who write for assistance to Catalyst, 6 East 82nd Street, New York City, New York 10028.

Women should also avail themselves of the free services offered by the subdivisions of state and federal departments of labor. Computerized job-data banks and, if you are lucky, staff members at these offices can often be of real help and speed up the job-hunting process.

The following directories provide comprehensive listings, by state, of counseling, educational, and/or placement services:

The New York Times Guide to Continuing Education in America (New York: Quadrangle Books, 1973). Available from publisher at 10 East 53rd Street, New York, N.Y. 10017.

U.S. Department of Labor, *Continuing Education Programs and Services for Women* (Washington, D.C.: Government Printing Office, 1971). Available from local Government Printing Office Bookstores or from the Superintendent of Documents, GPO, Washington, D.C. 20402.

Directory of Counseling Services (Washington, D.C.: International Association of Counseling Services, Inc., n.d.). Available from publisher at 1607 New Hampshire Avenue, N.W., Washington, D.C. 20009.

Appendix B: The Worksheet

The following is taken from *The Next Step*, a booklet put out by the Radcliffe Institute for Independent Study:

The worksheet provides a a framework for summarizing experiences, examining the beliefs and goals influencing one's choices, and evaluating abilities and skills. Although the answers are for personal use – *for clarifying, for planning, for recollecting forgotten experiences – the act of writing them down may be a useful preliminary to preparing a résumé. The résumé, in turn, is a prerequisite in any search for a job. After the worksheet is finished, it may be useful to look at it objectively, noting which replies seem superficial, and analyzing what short-term plans and long-range goals are suggested by the answers . . .*

This worksheet is for women who are uncertain about the direction they wish to take in making a next step. Many, of course, have clearly defined plans. But others share the feelings of the woman who said: "I know I want to do something, but I don't know what. I shift from plan to plan. One day I want to continue my education and get a graduate degree. Another day I'm certain I only want to work in some secure little niche that is not too demanding. I'm not really certain what field I wish to continue in, and I don't know what to do next. How do I go about finding out?"

. . . The worksheet questions can be a guide for organizing random thoughts and goals. They can be used as a basis for a continuing

group discussion, using these questions as a foundation for an extended examination of backgrounds and interests. Women who have difficulty getting started may be able to persuade a friend or two to answer the worksheet questions at the same time, and perhaps meet later to discuss their answers with each other. The woman who is genuinely interested in planning ahead will find it most helpful to write out her answers carefully.*

One word of caution: Consider your state of mind when working on this questionnaire. Don't tackle it at a time of extreme anguish. Wait till you have peace of mind.

WORKSHEET

Facts:

1. In what state of life are you?
   What are your personal commitments?
   What are your present time commitments?
   Do you have any children and if so, are they . . .

   a. Preschool children?
   b. School-age children?
   c. School-age children including adolescents?
   d. College-age children?
   e. All away from home?
   f. A combination of these? Specify.

   Are you likely to have responsibility for sick or aged parents or extended family?

2. List all your previous educational experience, giving names of schools and institutions, years of attendance, degrees, and honors. Include continuing and adult education courses.

3. List all your previous work experience. Describe thoroughly; start with the present and work backward. Include dates.

4. List any volunteer work in which you have participated and what you did. What did you most enjoy? And what did you dislike?

5. Have you any hobbies?

6. What sports do you like? In which do you participate?

7. Have you other special interests not taken into account?

Analyzing and Planning:

8. What do you like to read about in newspapers and magazines? What topics are interesting or exciting to you?

9. How would you categorize and describe your aptitudes, your talents and skills? What do others see as your strengths? Optional: Try writing a letter of recommendation for yourself.

10. What kind of leadership do you enjoy giving? Under what kind of leadership do you work best?

11. What did you most like to do in your education and your work? Did you prefer working with people or on projects? Do you like research or presentation? Individuals or groups? Responsibility or a clearly defined unit of work? With what ages do you like working? Children, men or women? Or do you not have a clearly defined preference?

12. Would you rather do *anything* for a cause you believe in or would you prefer to perform a particular function regardless of the employing agency?

13. What are your beliefs about community responsibility and service?

14.   *a.* If you could make charitable gifts what areas would you choose for allocation?

    b. Can you see yourself making a personal financial sacrifice for a cause you strongly believe in?

15. What are the major decisions facing you?

16. What are your goals and aims for the next year? The next 5 years? The next 20 years?

More Facts and Logistics:

17. If married:
    a. What are your husband's needs of you?
    b. What do you anticipate these needs will be in future decades?
    c. How does he view your future plans?

18. If you have children:
    a. What are their needs now in terms of your time, energy, and emotional involvement?
    b. What do you anticipate their future needs will be?
    c. Do your children have specific interests or problems that

you wish to share with them, or with which they need your help?

   d. If old enough, what suggestions can they offer you towards long term planning?

19. What, if any, are your arrangements for help at home and/or with children?

20. What are your projected vacation schedules?

21. What do you consider your major conflicts, those within yourself or those placed on you by outside forces?

22. When do you work best? Any particular season? Any particular time of day?

23. How would you describe your energy level?

24. What can you reject? What do you *not* want to consider?

25. Can you envision working as one half of a team, i.e., share responsibilities and hours with a partner? (This could be at any level including an executive position.)

Appendix C: Résumés, References, Portfolios

Before applying for any job, paid or volunteer, it is a good idea to prepare a résumé and have it ready to send out when needed. A job-winning résumé is comprehensive and attractively set up. This takes time and planning and is done well in advance of applying for work.

Quoting again from *The Next Step*:

Among the most difficult problems the mature woman faces when preparing her résumé are the selection and evaluation of the volunteer activities she wishes to include. A woman may be well advised to mention only her most important jobs, or those that have most relevance to the job she is seeking. If she wishes to demonstrate interest and involvement in one or more areas, she might group her volunteer experiences according to the type of activity (politics, education, welfare). If she wishes to show competence in a type of task, she might group her activities according to the motivations that led her to undertake them:

1.   *activities she participated in because of her children;*
2.   *those she took part in because of her interest in civic affairs;*
3.   *work done for its own sake which gave her experience related to her future goals.*

. . .Volunteer responsibilities had best be defined to prospective employers by such brief statements as these:

"Devised and put into operation new record system for . . ."
"Wrote brochures and letters for campaign to . . ."
"Served as chairman of committee to set up personnel practices for . . ."
"Did research on survey to . . ."

A résumé not only tells one's story succinctly, but it may also state or imply current employment goals. A woman as a volunteer may have assumed a higher level of responsibility than an employer can offer a beginner in his organization, particularly in a part-time job. In stating her experience, she will not wish to appear "overqualified" for jobs in which she might be interested. One way of handling this is to state in a brief sentence or paragraph what her short term and long term goals are. Or she might describe her previous experience in terms of attributes she has demonstrated: for example, competence in organization, facility with figures, skill in oral or written expression, ability to follow through, flexibility, and so forth. (Or this information may be presented in a covering letter or interview.)*

References: Keep personal and professional recommendations on file and ready to go out on short notice. Do not fail to ask for references relating to any volunteer job you may have held. Frequently, your college placement office will keep your references on file. Keep them updated.

Portfolios: If it is appropriate in your case, have a portfolio ready showing examples of your work in art, writing, or design. A few choice samples demonstrating your ability in the kind of work you are applying for are sufficient.

*White, Albro, and Skinner, eds., The Next Step (Cambridge, 1964), pp. 111-112.

Preparing a Résumé

A résumé is the conventional means of introducing yourself to prospective employers. As you will note in the material below, the form is a relatively simple one, but it is a *form* requiring specific techniques.

A Few Basic Principles:

1. The résumé is intended to be something more than a routine employment application form.

2. *Brevity* is important, but not at the expense of accuracy and completeness. If you have had considerable experience, you will need considerable space in which to describe it. For most persons seeking first full-time jobs, one page will be sufficient. An individual with several years of work experience will need two, and possibly three, pages.

3. Although the résumé may be looked upon as a selling device, it is primarily a factual document. It should point up your qualifications for a particular kind of work, but should under no circumstances exaggerate them.

4. *Generally the people who will be reviewing your résumé are highly trained in assessing candidates for employment.* They are not easily swayed by eye-catching gimmicks or elaborately original design. Almost invariably they will react negatively to glowing descriptions of how a person is prepared to reorganize the company. Use your energies instead in developing a logical, modest, well-phrased, and concise presentation.

5. Before you are ready to write a résumé, you will have to assess carefully your individual talents, abilities, and interests. Do this in a methodical fashion. *The more thoroughly you do this now, the less time you will waste in locating exactly the right spot for you.**

*Adapted from *Ginn's Guide to Writing Résumés and Sample Objectives*, copyright 1973 by the President and Fellows of Harvard University.

Drafting Your Copy. As you will note in looking over the two model résumés at the end of this Appendix, the following items should properly be included:

Vital Statistics: This should include your name, address, and telephone number.

Job Objective: The job objective is optional but useful to include. Included on the page preceding the two sample résumés is a list of sample job objectives. If formulating a job objective catapults you into existential crisis, then leave it out of the résumé and move on to the other sections. If you intend to apply for a variety of unrelated jobs, omit the job objective.

Education: In discussing your education include some description of both your academic work and your extracurricular activities. You may wish to describe more major activities in your work experience section — these experiences would be those which you felt were especially important whether they were paid or not. If you had special courses which prepare you for your job objective, mention them.

Work Experience: Your work experience need *not* be paid to be significant and important to the employer. If you have no work experience that you consider significant in itself or significant to your job objective, use the space to expand your discussion of your education. It really isn't very important to talk about marginally relevant summer jobs like packing groceries or being a lifeguard, especially if you feel that your course work or some volunteer work was more rewarding in terms of your own personal growth. The employer is interested in work you found challenging and important to your own growth.

Personal Background: Your personal background section offers the opportunity to raise issues or activities you feel are important to anyone who wishes to know who you are. Your home town, parental background, marital status, health, sex, age, etc., can be introduced here if you feel it is important. In many states, including Massachusetts, you *must omit* age, date of birth, place of birth, religion, sex, race, color, national origin, ancestry, and photographs in order to conform to the Fair Practice Law.

Study the models to get the feel of the special telegraphic style of writing and the section-by-section record of the facts of your own story. Where possible, avoid the use of the personal pronoun. Bear in mind continually that your reader wants primarily an accurate picture of what you have accomplished thus far in life.

Don't worry about length in your first draft. Write down everything that could reasonably be considered relevant to a particular section. Then, picking your words and phrases carefully, prune it down so that it contains in the fewest words possible a reasonable, accurate picture.

Your Final Layout. In setting up your final copy, remember that your format should accomplish two things. First, your résumé should *appear* attractive, easy to read, well organized, and business like. Pay due attention to underscorings, capitalization, paragraphing, and the like. Provide adequate margins, and use "white space" judiciously.

Your résumé should be designed in such a way that the reader can readily find any particular information that she or he may seek without being forced to read lines and lines of copy. The marginal index system followed in the two models is designed to accomplish this.

A clean multilith or photo-offset process is recommended. Have it prepared by electric typewriter and reproduced on good quality paper. Always present the printer with typed copy, spaced exactly the way you want it to appear. It is generally a good idea to check the galley or stencil yourself for misspellings, typographical errors, and spacing.

Sample Job Objectives for Your Résumé

Editorial, research, or personnel assistant in an organization concerned with social change — especially where an analytical approach, broad writing and speaking ability, and a major concern with organizational problem solving are needed to assure effective planning and follow-through and the reliable development of reports, studies, and programs.

Improvement of Personnel Organization: Assistant to executive concerned with improved personnel administration — especially where there is a need for development of policies and procedures to assure higher productivity and morale along with lower costs and turnover.

To work in accounting, sales, management information systems, or personnel in an international firm, with the opportunity to transfer to Greece or Italy.

To work in the transportation industry in the areas of finance, marketing, research, and program planning, especially where self-motivation, hard work, and a desire to assume responsibility as fast as I can effectively discharge it will be recognized by rapid advancement.

To work in the area of editorial research and writing for an international business or research organization. Special areas of interest include urban economics, technological innovation, analysis of the problems of Third World nations.

Broad interest in the area of social service and social change. Specifically, to obtain a position in which my ability to write, speak, and work well with other people will be exercised in working with community people around issues of transportation, adequate delivery of city services, welfare rights, or health rights.

My interest in working directly with people leads me to an interest in working with any agency providing direct services in the area of health, mental health, and rehabilitation.

Desire for solution of this nation's housing crisis leads me to seek employment with a general contractor or housing developer with the objective of gaining skills in the planning and construction of single- and multiple-unit housing in the Northwest.

Past success as a writer-editor leads me to seek a position with a newspaper, small television station, or publishing house assuming responsibility for copywriting and editing of nonfiction material. I am primarily interested in sharpening my skills as a reporter and scholar of contemporary history.

My interest and desire in working with children lead me to seek employment with day-care centers, private schools, curriculum designers, and children's toymakers. Skills in carpentry and pottery help me to help my students gain increased awareness of working with their hands as well as with their minds.

Two Sample Résumés

CHRISTINE ROBIN

23 Hyde Street
Apartment 204
Somerville, MA 02316
(617) 492-0611

Job Objective

I wish to work as a writer, researcher, and general editor with an employer whose interests are community service and social welfare.

Education

University of Illinois   B.S. Ed.
Urbana, Illinois 68204   June 1969

I concentrated in education — teaching art at the primary level. While I enjoyed working with small children and teaching art generally, my first love was writing. I worked as assistant editor of the campus newspaper during my junior and senior years. I helped Professor Jules Henry edit his textbook *Teaching Art: A Cognitive Development Approach*, and my work is acknowledged in his Preface.

Work Experience

Quality Educational Development Co.   Researcher
Brighton, MA 09845   Supervisor: Jane Moore

I worked from March 1970 to June 1971. I worked as an elementary school arts curriculum writer. I wrote the "Modeling Clay" and "Scissors/Paste" divisions of a curriculum for third-grade students. The curriculum was successfully marketed to thirty-five school systems.

Volunteer Experience

Since 1970, I have been working in an adult literacy program, mostly with Spanish-speaking immigrants, two nights a week.

Travel Experience

I travelled from June 1969 until January 1970 throughout Mexico. I speak Spanish fluently and gained great insight into the oppressive conditions of the farm workers near the Texas and New Mexico borders. I saw the problems of the marginal economy and the total lack of basic services including education for literacy.

Personal Background

I was born in Chicago, Illinois, of working class Black parents. I attended public schools in Chicago and worked while in high school as a case aide in a Catholic Charities bureau. I was married in June 1971 and have one child, Talitha.

References

My personal file is available from the Career Services Office, 22 Holmand Hall, University of Illinois, Urbana, Illinois 68204.

LILLY JANE ROWLAND-SMYTHE

38 The Pines
Osterville, Massachusetts 03249
(617) 445-8932

Education

University of Massachusetts   B.A. *Cum laude*
Amherst, Massachusetts 04519   June 1948

I concentrated in educational psychology with strong minors in
English literature, sociology, and statistics. I was secretary of
the senior class and president of my sorority. I had strong
interests in working with other people in various campus organizations and off-campus community service projects.

Work Experience

Abbot Memorial Library   Assistant Director
Emerson College   Readers' Services
Boston, Massachusetts 03124   Supervisor: Helen Lotto

I worked from July 1954 until April 1973. I began as a cataloging
assistant and worked my way to my final position as assistant
director of readers' services, which meant I was responsible for
assisting students and faculty in their use of the library
facilities. I reorganized the reserve library policies and procedures to encourage access to our collection while maintaining
its security. I supervised the work of the staff and students who
worked the reference desks and catalog assistance station. I
established the microfilm collection and reading room.

Lycée Charles Bonaparte   English Teacher
Sceaux, France   Principal: Henri Meiro

I worked from September 1950 until June 1954. My work was to
teach English and French to students of French and American
parents. The school was private with a largely middle-class
student body. My time in France afforded me the opportunity

to refine my interests in 17th Century French Masters. I published two papers on the painting of Nicolas Boileau-Despréaux relating his art to his poetry. They appear in the Fall and Winter 1952 issues of *The Journal of French Art.*

Boston Public Schools   School Psychologist
Boston, Massachusetts   Superintendent: William O'Leary

I worked from September 1948 until June 1950. I organized the first tests of reading and verbal skills administered to third graders throughout the system. I cataloged the tests and measures available to teachers and organized the test-request procedures still used in the Boston Public Schools.

Personal Background

I was born in England and emigrated to this country at age two. I am a naturalized citizen. My mother was a French actress, and my father taught mathematics at Boston College.

Appendix D: Volunteer and Agency Guide Lines: Model Agreements and Regulations

This section should be read in association with chapter 6, "The Idea of the Volunteer Professional." Providing a detailed set of guidelines for volunteers as well as for agencies, it attempts to define the responsibilities of both parties. These guidelines were prepared for the Boston Voluntary Action Center by a subcommittee of its volunteer board in close cooperation with the Civic Center and Clearing House, Inc.

The second part of this section contains the model agreements worked out by "Call for Action." Also included is a list of the regulations on the deductibility of expenses incurred by volunteers, discussed in chapter 6.

While the guidelines and model agreements are not yet in common use, they represent an effort to help professionalize "volunteer" status. In an attempt to foster greater awareness of the role of the volunteer professional, they also signal to all concerned that the role of the volunteer is a serious one and should carry with it the same kind of commitment as that expected of a regular paid employee.

GUIDELINES

For Organizations, Agencies, and Institutions
Employing Volunteers

It is necessary to:

● designate a coordinator of volunteers to serve as a liaison between the community, the volunteer, and the organization.

● discuss with staff how volunteers can be placed to extend and improve services within time and budget limits without displacing paid workers.

● provide written job descriptions when possible, outlining the time and skills needed and the duties to be performed.

● give prospective volunteers the same careful placement attention as the paid employees. Volunteers should not be accepted who are unsuited to the work available.

● provide orientation and initial and refresher training when necessary to stimulate and increase volunteer skills and interests.

● establish and communicate clearly defined lines of supervision so volunteers know to whom they are responsible.

●maintain appropriate records of volunteer service.

● consider reimbursing the volunteer for out-of-pocket expenses when resources are available and the request has been made.

● encourage volunteers who are ready for a new experience or more responsibility to seek new assignments within the organization; otherwise refer them to a volunteer placement office.

GUIDELINES

For Volunteers

Volunteers are people who give of their time in service to the community. In addition, they have a unique opportunity to serve as interpreters between the community and the agency.

Volunteers should:

• carefully choose the area in which they wish to work. Jobs suited to their interests and abilities are likely to be most rewarding.

• realistically estimate the amount of time they have to give. Most volunteer assignments require a minimum of three hours a week. Having made the time commitment, it should be honored.

• expect to arrive at their assignment at the agreed time. If they must be absent, they should call as soon as possible.

• be clear as to what their roles and duties are, and they may request written job descriptions. Volunteers should expect continued guidance and direction.

• expect to participate in orientation sessions, and they are urged to attend training programs. If volunteers find their time is not well spent, they should discuss the situation with the person in charge.

• respect the principle of confidentiality and follow the same ethical standards expected of all staff members.

• approach their working situation with open minds. If there is any procedure they do not understand or agree with, they should ask questions. There may be good reason for it, or it may be time for change.

Model Agreement

The Volunteer Professional Agrees:

To work a specified number of hours each week on a schedule acceptable to the agency.

To become thoroughly familiar with the agency's policies and procedures, both written and verbal, set forth by the agency for volunteer professionals.

To be prompt and reliable in reporting for scheduled work, and to provide the agency with an accurate record of hours worked by signing in or out when entering or leaving.

To notify the agency's director of volunteers if unable to work as scheduled. This will be done as early as possible to permit reassignment of another volunteer professional if necessary.

To attend orientation and training sessions as scheduled, and to undertake continuing education when provided by the agency to maintain continuing competence.

To respect the function of the agency's paid staff and contribute fully toward maintaining a smooth working relationship between paid staff and volunteer professionals.

To realize that, while the agency and its paid staff welcome questions and suggestions from volunteer professionals, it is not the purpose of the volunteer professionals to supplant the staff. In particular, volunteer professionals will not seek paid staff positions with the agency.

To carry out assignments in good spirit and to seek the assistance of the director of volunteers in any situation requiring special guidance.

To consult with the director of volunteers before assuming any new responsibilities affecting the agency.

To accept the agency's right to dismiss any volunteer professional for poor performance, including poor attendance.

To notify the director of volunteers in writing at least three weeks in advance of any resignation or requests for leave of absence from the agency's volunteer professional program.

To exercise caution when acting on the agency's behalf in any situation, and to protect the confidentiality of all information relating to the agency.

To abide by the decisions of the volunteer advisory council on any matters in dispute between the agency and any volunteer professional.

Model Agreement

The Agency Agrees:

To provide a director of volunteers who will be responsible for the hiring, firing, orientation, training, and supervision of all volunteer professionals. The director will be available to guide and assist volunteer professionals during their scheduled working hours, and will serve as the link between the volunteer professionals and the agency's paid staff.

To furnish a written job description for each position open to volunteer professionals, with appropriate information concerning desirable experience, skills, and education.

To train volunteer professionals to a level that will permit them to begin their work confidently.

To continue the volunteer professionals' training, either within the agency or elsewhere, to whatever extent is necessary to maintain continuing competence.

To provide volunteer professionals with working conditions equal to those of paid employees doing similar work, including space, equipment, and supplies.

To make written evaluations of volunteer professionals' performance on the job at suitable and regular intervals, including the number of hours worked.

To offer volunteer professionals promotion to more responsible jobs within the agency's volunteer program.

To include volunteer professionals in agency staff conferences when possible and otherwise to promote full understanding among the volunteer professionals of the agency's working and decisions.

To reimburse volunteer professionals directly for out-of-pocket expenses required by their work and to provide indirect benefits (such as day care) when these are available to agency employees.

To provide volunteer professionals with a certificate of service for satisfactory work and to supplement the certificate with a detailed recommendation if requested by a volunteer professional applying for a job elsewhere.

To maintain adequate public liability and other insurance coverage for volunteer professionals during those hours when they are actually working for the agency.

To indemnify volunteer professionals for any cost, damage, or expense arising from their activities authorized by the agency.

To create a volunteer advisory council consisting of the agency's executive director, the director of volunteers, one other agency staff member, and two volunteer professionals, and to schedule regular meetings of this council.

Legislation/regulations:
>   . . . of concern to volunteers and
>   voluntarism*

> *Regulations on the Deductibility of Expenses Incurred by Volunteers*
>   At times the individual volunteer may have questions as to the Internal Revenue Service's attitude about the deductibility of out-of-pocket expenses incurred in the performance of charitable volunteer activity. Mr. Wilson Fadley, a spokesman for the IRS, informed the National Center for Voluntary Action that volunteer coordinators and trainers could be most useful in explaining the existence and means of claiming these deductions. Simply translated, the IRS regulations covering this subject are as follows:
>   *The cost of transportation* from a volunteer's home to where he serves is deductible.
>   *Reasonable costs for meals and lodging,* if a volunteer is away

---

Volunteer Action Leadership (Washington, D.C.: National Center for Volunteer Action), November-December 1973, p. 13.

from home while donating his service to a qualified organization, are deductible.

But personal expenses for sightseeing and entertainment, as well as travel, meals, and lodging expenses for an accompanying spouse, children, etc. are not deductible.

The cost of attending a religious convention as a duly chosen representative of one's church or synagogue is deductible.

The cost and upkeep of uniforms that have no general utility and are required to be worn while performing donated services are deductible.

Unreimbursed expenses directly connected with and solely attributable to voluntary service performed for one's church or synagogue are deductible.

Use of personal auto – Volunteers may deduct out-of-pocket expenses for gas and oil which are used for services rendered to a charitable organization.

Or, if a volunteer does not wish to deduct his gas and oil expenses, he may use a standard rate of 7c per mile to determine his contribution. Under this method, parking fees and tolls are deductible — in addition to the 6c per mile.

However — the costs of auto insurance and normal depreciation are *not deductible.* Nor is a pro rata portion of the general repair and maintenance cost of a volunteer's auto which is used occasionally for volunteer work.

Per diem allowance — If a volunteer performs a gratuitous service for a charitable organization and receives a per diem allowance to cover reasonable travel expenses, including meals and lodging, while away from home in the performance of such duties . . .

the allowance *to the extent it exceeds actual travel expenses* is regarded as *income;*

but travel expenses *to the extent they exceed the allowance* are deductible.

Mr. Fadley advises interested volunteers to obtain a copy of IRS Publication No. 526, "Income Tax Deductions for Contributions," from their local IRS offices. If questions arise, he suggests they contact their local offices for answers, particularly the Office of Taxpayer Assistance.

If an IRS office is not conveniently accessible, aid and answers may be obtained by calling the IRS toll-free. The number is listed in all telephone directories.

Appendix E: Key Voluntary Sector Umbrella Groups of North America: Selected List

Prepared by the Center for a Voluntary Society
This list draws partly on the NCVA (National Center for Voluntary Action) Clearinghouse *Green Sheets* but adds several other organizations not included there. We attempt to give a selective overview of coordinating groups in terms of the full sociopolitical spectrum from conservative to radical. *All* of this spectrum exists and is having an important impact on our society. The very existence of such a wide spectrum of private philanthropic, voluntary, nongovernment, nonprofit coordinating groups is an affirmation of First Amendment freedoms of association, assembly, and dissent. To ignore any part of this spectrum in attempting to understand private philanthropy and the voluntary sector is implicitly to deny a palpable reality that is "out there," whether one likes it or not.

ACTION
806 Connecticut Avenue
Washington, D.C. 20625

Government umbrella agency administering several major federal volunteer and quasi-volunteer programs — Peace

Corps, VISTA, Foster Grandparents, RSVP, SCORE, ACE, and
National Student Volunteer Program. Promotes volunteerism
at home and abroad. Gives limited grants and supplies some
program development assistance to local agencies upon
request. Recruits volunteers for all above programs.

Alternative Press Index
Radical Research Center
Bag Service 2500
Postal Station E
Toronto, Ontario, Canada

Provides a quarterly index to some 90 underground and
radical newspapers and magazines in the United States and
Canada. Published by the Radical Research Center, the index is
prepared in a format similar to *The Reader's Guide to Periodical
Literature*. The index and the center constitute a clearinghouse
for change-oriented voluntary recruitment and placement activities in North America.

American Association of
  Fund-Raising Counsel
500 Fifth Avenue
New York, New York 10036

This is a "trade" organization of profit-making, fund-raising
counseling firms. The association provides an information
clearinghouse and serves as a forum for the exchange of ideas
and experiences among firms engaged in managing, planning,
and consulting for fund-raising efforts to finance hospitals,
educational, religious, community fund, and other nonprofit
institutions. They publish *Giving — USA* annually and also
produce a semimonthly publication, *Bulletin*.

American Association of Volunteer
  Services Coordinators
18 South Michigan Avenue, Room 602
Chicago, Illinois 60603

Membership organization open to salaried coordinators of volunteer programs and their assistants. Supplies professional administrators of volunteer programs with an established plan for the certification of volunteer services coordinators, regional and national activities, a newsletter, tape library, and current professional information. Promotes volunteer administration as a profession, development of volunteer services programs, fair standards for the utilization of volunteers, development of higher educational training for volunteer administrators, and the exchange among membership of creative and useful ideas.

American Council of Voluntary Agencies
  for Foreign Service, Inc.
200 Park Avenue South
New York, New York 10003

Established in 1944, the American Council of Voluntary Agencies for Foreign Service, a consulting, coordinating, and planning agency, assures the most effective use of American contributions for the assistance of people overseas. Its 42 members, American voluntary agencies engaged in overseas service programs, coordinate their activities nationally and internationally among themselves, with nonmember agencies and with government and international organizations. Three standing committees of the council deal with areas of concern to its members: Development Assistance, Material Resources, and Migration and Refugee Affairs. Ad hoc committees on geographical areas of particular concern are provided as needed. The council has received grants and other funds from foundations and the U.S. government for specific projects and services beyond the needs of the regular council membership

Since 1955, under contract with AID, the Council has operated the Technical Assistance Information Clearing House — a center of information on the socioeconomic development programs of U.S. nonprofit organizations abroad. It makes its source materials available to interested persons for study and research; and it gives current information about development assistance with particular reference to the resources and concerns of the private, voluntary, nonprofit sector through publications and a daily inquiry service.

American Society of Association Executives
1101 16th St.
Washington, D.C.

This is a professional society of paid executives of trade, professional, and business associations. The society serves as a national forum concerning the goals, functions, and activities of associations; the basic principles of association organization; and the policies, methods, and techniques of association management. The society seeks to develop and promote professional standards of association executives. The society conducts research and educational programs for association executives. A reference library is maintained, including statistics, reports, and surveys. The society also provides placement, guidance, and consultation services. Publications include the monthly *Association Management* and the annual *Who's Who in Association Management*.

American Society of Directors of
    Volunteer Services, of the
American Hospital Association
840 North Lake Shore Drive
Chicago, Illinois 60611

Membership organization open to persons employed or recognized by the administration of a health care institution as having major or continuing responsibility for the volunteer services programs within that institution. Strives to increase the knowledge and skills of individual members and to provide a channel of communication among them. Also attracts new members of the profession and seeks to retain skilled members. Provides publications and conducts an annual educational meeting in conunction with a business meeting of the society.

Association of Voluntary Action Scholars
Box G-55, McGuinn Hall 504B
Boston College
Chestnut Hill, Massachusetts 02167

Interdisciplinary and interprofessional organization seeking to foster the dissemination and application of social science knowledge about voluntary action. Membership open to academics, voluntary action leaders, and individual volunteers interested both in voluntary action research and the practical application of that research. Provides a scholarly *Journal of Voluntary Action Research* to members, a newsletter, and informal channels of communication among scholars and voluntary activists.

Association of Volunteer Bureaus
P.O.Box 125
801 North Fairfax Street
Alexandria, Virginia 22313

Membership organization open to local volunteer recruitment and placement centers willing to take responsibility in the community planning process for coordination, development of standards, and consultation to agencies and citizen groups on all matters of citizen participation, and to recruit and refer individual volunteers. The AVB maintains a national library primarily of "loan folders" on the generic areas of volunteerism and publishes a newsletter to keep their membership current on matters pertinent to the field.

The Center for a Voluntary Society
1100 17th Street, N.W., Suite 711
Washington, D.C. 20036

Stimulates and performs basic and applied research on voluntary action; collects, synthesizes, analyzes, publishes, and disseminates relevant research information and practical experience both to scholars and to practitioners in the field. The center engages in policy interpretation and stimulates discussion of issues vital to voluntarism; develops methods of evaluation for the voluntary sector; holds conferences, workshops, seminars, and informal discussions with practitioners, professionals, and scholars; consults with voluntary organizations regarding their goals, policies, operations, and evaluation systems, and has aided in the development of the independent Association of Voluntary Action Scholars.

Council on Foundations
888 7th Avenue
New York, New York 10019

A membership organization which seeks to "provide a common meeting ground and service for foundations administering charitable funds for public purposes and to encourage broader understanding of the community foundation concept." Through national offices and a field service, the organization provides advice to active and prospective foundations. Membership includes community, family, company, and other foundations. Publishes an annual *Report on Status,* an annual *Conference Proceedings,* and a *Handbook on Community Foundations in the U.S. and Canada.*

Foundation Center
888 7th Avenue
New York, New York 10019

The Foundation Library Center was established as an educational organization through an initial grant from Carnegie Corporation of New York. Its purpose is to collect, organize, and disseminate reports and information about foundations organized and operated exclusively for charitable, scientific, literary, or educational purposes which are tax exempt. It is also concerned with the development and maintenance of sound standards for reporting by such foundations and to assist them in making such reports available to the public. The Library Center acquired books, reports, and files on philanthropy originally accumulated by the Russell Sage Foundation. They publish *The Foundation Directory* and a bimonthly *Foundation News*.

The Source Collective
P.O. Box 21066
Washington, D.C. 20009

A change-oriented collective of young people, producing national directories of alternative and radical voluntary groups and resources. Two catalogues have been published — Communications and Housing — describing hundreds of voluntary organizations, books, pamphlets, tapes, and films. A health catalog is under way. Other publications include booklets on women on campus, and day care. Source also answers individual information requests and is developing an Organizer's Resource Center.

The National Assembly of National Voluntary Health and
    Welfare Organizations
345 East 46th Street
New York, New York 10017

Formed in 1967 from a merger of the National Social Welfare Assembly and the National Association for Social Policy and Development. The assembly was reorganized as an association of 300 citizens, half at large and half from associated organizations. The assembly's basic purpose has been the initiation, evaluation, development, and advancement of sound, progressive social policies and organization programs. It seeks to bring about change, where needed, in existing governmental and voluntary policies and programs. A research center supports these aims, conducting studies and analyzing the applicability of research done elsewhere. It provides conceptual models with transplant value and capacity for escalation and expansion. In conjunction with the center, a series of university-based satellites focus on the same sorts of problems where they possess competence in a given area of assembly interest. A Washington staff provides lobbying efforts. The assembly publishes a monthly Newsletter. Recently, there has been a shift in emphasis to being more of a convener and service organization for its constituent groups.

National Center for Voluntary Action
1785 Massachusetts Avenue, N.W.
Washington, D.C. 20036

A private, nonprofit agency established in 1970 as the result of a Nixon campaign commitment, the center promotes volunteerism nationally. It has developed a National Clearinghouse which publishes resource materials for voluntary action programs ("the Green Sheets") and has a file of over 5,000 prototype programs utilizing volunteers in all areas from health to education. It operates a yearly National Volunteer Awards Program and has developed a national network of Voluntary Action Centers (volunteer bureaus). VACs are locally formed and based, and concentrate on coordinating, planning, and developing volunteer programs locally through the recruitment and placement of volunteers (mainly in social service, health, and welfare settings).

National Information Bureau
419 Park Avenue South
New York, New York 10016

This organization provides a reporting and advisory service about national and international fund-raising nonprofit organizations that solicit contributions annually. This group evaluates each philanthropic organization in terms of NIB standards of origin, purpose, program, leadership, and finances. A newsletter is published on an irregular basis.

National Information Center on Volunteerism, Inc.
1221 University Avenue
Boulder, Colorado 80302

Established to encourage, promote, and increase knowledge of volunteer activities related but not restricted to courts and other criminal justice programs, the center provides program information from extensive files it has collected. The files include information on programs, manuals, handbooks, and other practitioner-oriented publications. The center operates a variety of training programs and conferences. The center also publishes a quarterly newsletter designed to keep readers informed of meetings, conferences, workshops, opinions of experts, issues, and challenges affecting volunteerism.

National School Volunteer Program, Inc.
450 North Grand Avenue
Rm. G 114
Los Angeles, California 90051

A membership organization open to directors and coordinators of school volunteer programs with an associate membership open to anyone interested in or associated with a school volunteer program. The organization provides a newsletter and an annual conference to share expertise and experience and to improve communication among the growing school programs. The organization maintains a bibliography of resources for people inquiring about setting up new programs. It also encourages established programs to assist beginners located nearby.

United Way
801 North Fairfax Street
Alexandria, Virginia 22314

Founded in 1918, this organization includes all local United Funds, Community Chests, and Community Welfare Councils in 2200 communities of the United States. Serves members in their work of United Fund raising and in community planning for voluntary health, welfare, and recreation agencies. Maintains a placement service for people wishing to enter paid community organization practice in its member groups. Compiles statistical information on fund raising and health and welfare services. Publishes a monthly magazine — *Community*.

Vocations for Social Change
4911 Telegraph Avenue
Oakland, California 94609

This is one of the oldest social-change – oriented movement information centers, providing a clearinghouse of opportunities to work for change in society. VSC publishes a bimonthly booklet *Workforce* — listing many job possibilities in alternative institutions, voluntary groups, and radical projects. Each issue focuses on one area (e.g., health, labor organizing, education) and includes descriptions of basic radical resource groups, brief articles, and bibliographies. Local centers in about 40 cities offer individual job counseling and are often information clearinghouses.

Volunteers in Probation
A Division of the National Council
    on Crime and Delinquency
200 Washington Square Plaza
Royal Oak, Michigan 48067

Membership organization which assists in the development of volunteer programs with courts and correctional institutions by furnishing — without cost — speakers, consultants, work-shops, demonstrations, films, tapes, and literature on court volunteer programs. Primary objectives of the organization are to stimulate citizen participation in the courts and corrections programs, to provide a channel of communication among exist-ing programs, and to develop state organizations to dissemi-nate the concept of the use of volunteers in these areas.

Appendix F: Resource Network of National Associations of Professional Women*

Adult Education Association (AEA)
Commission on the Status of Women in Adult Education
Chairperson: Dr. Beverly Cassara
                      10421 Courthouse Drive
                      Fairfax, Virginia 22030

American Anthropological Association (AAA)
Committee on the Status of Women in Anthropology
Chairperson: Professor Shirley Gorenstein
                      Department of Anthropology
                      Columbia University
                      New York, New York 10027

American Association of Immunologists (AAI)
Committee on the Status of Women (AAI has list of women
  members)
Chairperson: Dr. Helene C. Rauch
                      Department of Medical Microbiology
                      Stanford University School of Medicine
                      Stanford, California 94305

---

*Prepared for the Governor's Commission on the Status of Women, by
Elizabeth Garniss and Jessie Pearl Bailey (Boston, October 1973).
  Many of these organizations belong to the Federation of Organizations for
Professional Women, 828 Washington Street, Wellesley, Massachusetts 02181.

American Association of University Professors (AAUP)
Committee on the Status of Women in the Profession
Chairperson: Dr. Alice S. Rossi
                          Department of Sociology
                          Goucher College
                          Towson, Maryland 21204
                          AAUP Contact:Ms. Margaret Rumbarger
                                                Associate Secretary, AAUP
                                                One Dupont Circle
                                                Washington, D.C. 20036

American Chemical Society (ACS)
Women Chemists Committee
Chairperson: Ms. Helen M. Free
                          Ames Company
                          Miles Labs, Inc.
                          Elkhart, Indiana 46514

American College Personnel Association (ACPA)
Women's Task Force
Chairperson: Dr. Jane E. McCormick
                          Assistant to Vice-President
                             of Student Affairs
                          Penn State University
                          University Park, Pennsylvania 16802

American Historical Association (AHA)
Committee on Women Historians
Chairperson: Professor Patricia A. Graham
                          Barnard College
                          New York, New York 10027
                          Staff Liaison: Professor Dorothy Ross
                                                2914 33rd Place, N.W.
                                                Washington, D.C. 20003

Coordinating Committee on Women in the Historical Profession (CCWHP)

Chairperson: Dean Adele Simmons
             Dean of Student Affairs
             Princeton University
             Princeton, New Jersey 08540

American Library Association (ALA)
Social Responsibilities Round Table (SRRT)
Task Force on the Status of Women
Chairperson: Ms. Michelle Rudy
             403 Waldron
             Lafayette, Indiana 47409

American Philosophical Association (APA)
Subcommittee on Status of Women in the Profession
Chairperson: Professor Mary Motherskill
             Department of Philosophy
             Barnard College
             New York, New York 10027

American Physical Society
Committee on Women in Physics
Chairperson: Dr. Elizabeth Baranger
             Physics Department
             Massachusetts Institute of Technology
             Cambridge, Massachusetts 02139

American Political Science Association (APSA)
Committee on the Status of Women in the Profession
Chairperson: Dr. Ruth Silva
             Pennsylvania State University
             University Park, Pennsylvania 16802

Women's Caucus for Political Science (WCPS)
Chairperson: Dr. Evelyn P. Stevens
             Box 9099
             Pittsburgh, Pennsylvania 15224

American Psychological Association (APA)
Task Force on the Status of Women in Psychology

Chairperson: Dr. Helen Astin
             Director of Research
             University Research Corp.
             4301 Connecticut Avenue, N.W.
             Washington, D.C. 20008
             Staff Liaison: Dr. Tena Cummings, APA
                              1200 17th Street, N.W.
                              Washington, D.C. 20036

Association for Women in Psychology (AWP) is an independent group initially a caucus within APA

Editor: Dr. Leigh Marlowe
             Manhattan Community College
             180 West End Avenue
             New York, New York 10023

Public
Relations: Dr. Jo-Ann Evans Gardner
             726 St. James Street
             Pittsburgh, Pennsylvania 15232

American Society of Biological Chemists
Subcommittee on the Status of Women
Chairperson: Dr. Loretta Leive
             Building 4, Room 111
             National Institutes of Health
             Bethesda, Maryland 20014

American Society of Microbiology
Committee on the Status of Women Microbiologists
Chairperson: Dr. Mary Louise Robbins
             Medical School
             The George Washington University
             1339 H Street, N.W.
             Washington, D.C. 20005

American Society of Public Administration
Task Force on Women in Public Administration

Chairperson: Mrs. Joan Fiss Bishop
            Director of Career Services
            Wellesley College
            Wellesley, Massachusetts 02181

American Society of Training and Development (ASTD)
Women's Caucus, ASTD
Steering Committee:Dr. Shirley McCune
                    Center for Human Relations, NEA
                    1601 16th Street, N.W.
                    Washington, D.C. 20036
                    Ms. Althea Simmons
                    Director of Training, NAACP
                    200 E. 27th Street
                    New York, New York 10016

American Sociological Association (ASA)
Ad Hoc Committee on the Status of Women in Sociology
Chairperson: Dr. Elise Boulding
            Behavioral Science Institute
            University of Colorado
            Boulder, Colorado 80302

Sociologists for Women in Society (SWS) independent group
   formerly caucus
Chairperson: Dr. Alice Rossi
            Department of Sociology
            Goucher College
            Towson, Maryland 21204

American Speech and Hearing Association (ASHA)
Subcommittee on the Status of Women
Chairperson: Mrs. Dorothy K. Marge
            8011 Longbrook Road
            Springfield, Virginia 22152
Caucus on Status of Women in ASHA
Chairperson: Same as above

Association of American Geographers (AAG)
Committee on Women in Geography
Chairperson: Dr. Ann Larrimore
            Department of Geography
            University of Michigan
            Ann Arbor, Michigan 48104

Association of American Law Schools (AALS)
Women in the Legal Profession
Chairperson: Professor Ruth B. Ginsburg
            School of Law
            Columbia University
            435 West 116 Street
            New York, New York 10027

Association of Asian Studies (AAS)
Committee on the Status of Women
Chairperson: Professor Joyce K. Kallgren
            Center for Chinese Studies
            2168 Shattuck Avenue
            Berkeley, California 94705

Association of Women in Science (AWS)
Co-
Presidents: Dr. Judith G. Pool
            Stanford Medical School
            Stanford University
            Stanford, California 94305

            Dr. Neena B. Schwartz
            Department of Psychiatry
            College of Medicine
            University of Illinois at the Medical Center
            P.O. Box 6998
            Chicago, Illinois 60680

Graduate Women in Science (Sigma Delta Epsilon)
President: Dr. Hazel Metz Fox
            1231 N. 38th Street
            Lincoln, Nebraska 65503

Linguistic Society of America (LSA)
LSA Women's Caucus
Correspondents: Ms. Lynette Hirschman
                 Ms. Georgette Loup
                 162 W. Hansberry
                 Philadelphia, Pennsylvania 19144

Modern Language Association (MLA)
MLA Commission on the Status of Women in the Profession
Chairperson: Dr. Carol Ohmann
              Wesleyan University
              Middletown, Connecticut 06457

Women's Caucus of the MLA
President: Dr. Verna Wittrock
               Department of English
               Eastern Illinois University
               Charleston, Illinois 61920

National Council of Teachers of English (NCTE)
Women's Committee
Chairperson: Dr. Janet Emig
              Department of English
              Rutgers University
              New Brunswick, New Jersey 08903

National Education Association (NEA)
Women's Caucus
Chairperson: Mrs. Helen Bain
              1201 16th Street, N.W.
              Washington, D.C. 20036

National Vocational Guidance Association (NVGA)
NVGA Commission on the Occupational Status of Women
Chairperson: Mrs. Thelma C. Lennon
              Director, Pupil Personnel Services
              Department of Public Instruction
              Raleigh, North Carolina 27602

Professional Women's Caucus (PWC)
President: Ms. Sheila Tobias
              Assistant Provost of Wesleyan University
              Middletown, Connecticut 06457

Association of Women Mathematicians
Chairperson: Professor Mary W. Gray
             Department of Mathematics
             American University
             Washington, D.C. 20016

American Association of University Women
Chairperson: Dr. Ruth Oltman
             Staff Associate of Higher Education
             2401 Virginia Avenue, N.W.
             Washington, D.C. 20037

Association of American Colleges
Advisory Committee for the Project on the Status and Education of Women
Chairperson: Dr. Bernice Sandler
             1818 R Street, N.W.
             Washington, D.C. 20009

National Association of Women Deans and Counselors
Chairperson: Ms. Anna Rankin Harris
             1201 16th Street, N.W.
             Washington, D.C.

Association of Collegiate Schools of Architecture (ACSA)
Women Architects
Write to: ACSA
              1785 Massachusetts Avenue, N.W.
              Washington, D.C. 20036

Alliance of Women in Architecture
Write to: AWA
              18 E. 13th Street
              New York, New York 10003

Women Engineers, Scientists, Medical, and Paramedical
  Specialists
Biophysical Society and the Association of Women in Science
Write to: Dr. Marion Webster
           2226 Broadbranch Terrace
                              Washington, D.C. 20008

Women in Religious Studies
Women in Religion
Write To: Women's Caucus — Religious Studies
          Box 6309 Station B
          Vanderbilt University
          Nashville, Tennessee 37235

National Register of Scientific and Technical Personnel
National Science Foundation (number of scientists by sex,
  field, and work)
1800 G Street, N.W.
Washington, D.C. 20506

Boston Theological Institute
Women's Institute Placement Service (women qualified
  to teach theology)
45 Francis Avenue
Cambridge, Massachusetts 02138

Institute for College and University Administrators
American Council on Education (Women Academic Adminis-
  trators in Higher Ed.)
One Dupont Circle
Washington, D.C. 20036

Committee on Equality of Opportunity in Psychology
American Psychological Association (minorities and women
  in the field)
1200 17th Street, N.W.
Washington, D.C. 20036

Bibliography

Fortunately for the person interested in pursuing the subject of voluntarism, there exist several exhaustive and up-to-date bibliographies:

CVS-VOLINFLO Bibliography and Abstracts File, compiled by David Horton Smith, Richard D. Reddy, Burt R. Baldwin, et al. (Washington, D.C.: Center for a Voluntary Society, n.d.). This is a computer printout of the latest version of CVS's partially annotated, comprehensive bibliography of all known articles, books, and other documents related to voluntary action, whether scholarly or applied in orientation. The file is continuously updated. Materials are categorized by general topic areas, such as Health, Environment, Education, and so on. Available from CVS at 1785 Massachusetts Avenue, N.W., Washington, D.C. 20036.

General Voluntarism Annotated Bibliography: 1973, compiled by David Horton Smith, Marge Shultz, Barbara Marsh, and Cathy Orme (Washington, D.C.: Center for a Voluntary Society, May 1973). Available from CVS.

Voluntary Associations: Perspectives on the Literature, by Constance Smith and Anne Freedman (Cambridge: Harvard University Press, 1972). This is a survey of the literature on voluntary associations, with an annotated bibliography of over 600 items.

For listings of publications in the field of voluntarism you may also write to CVS (at the address above) and to the Clearinghouse of the National Center for Voluntary Action, 1785 Massachusetts Avenue, N.W., Washington, D.C. 20036. The latter list includes practical guides under different headings: Resource Group, Information and Referral, Program Evaluation, Organization and Administration in Volunteering, and Volunteer-Staff Relations.

Articles of current interest may be found in the *Journal of Voluntary Action Research*, a quarterly appearing in Washington, D.C. (first issued in 1972), edited by David Horton Smith and Richard D. Reddy, and published by the Association of Voluntary Action Scholars.

Part One

Bauer, Raymond, and Dan H. Fenn, Jr., *The Corporate Social Audit* (New York: Russell Sage Foundation, 1972).

Best, Fred, ed., *The Future of Work* (Englewood Cliffs, N.J.: Prentice-Hall, 1973).

Boals, Kay, "Getting Feminine Qualities into the Power Structure," in *University: A Princeton Quarterly*, No. 54, Fall 1972, pp. 6-12.

Buckley, Marie, *Breaking into Prison* (Boston: Beacon Press, 1974).

Cohen, Nathan E., ed., *The Citizen Volunteer: His Responsibility, Role, and Opportunity in Modern Society* (New York: Harper & Brothers, 1960).

Elbing, Alvar O., Herman Gadon, and John R. M. Gordon, "Flexible Working Hours: It's About Time," in *Harvard Business Review*, January/February, 1974, pp. 18-28, 33, 154-155.

Fenn, Dan H., Jr., "Executives as Community Volunteers," in *Harvard Business Review*, March/April 1971, pp. 4-16, 156-159.

Friedan, Betty, *The Feminine Mystique* (New York: W.W. Norton & Co., Inc., 1963 and New York: Dell Publishing Co., 1964).

Giele, Janet Zollinger, *Women and the Future*, a report to the Ford Foundation (unpublished).

Gold, Doris B., "Women and Voluntarism," in *Woman in Sexist Society*, edited by Vivian Gornick and Barbara K. Moran (New York: Basic Books, Inc., 1971), pp. 384-400.

Goldston, Eli, *The Quantification of Concern: Some Aspects of Social Accounting* (Pittsburgh: Carnegie Press, Carnegie Mellon University, 1974).

————,"Executive Sabbaticals: About to Take Off?" in *Harvard Business Review*, September/October 1973, pp. 57-68, reprints available.

Goodman, Natalie C., *A Reconsideration of the Concepts of Leisure and Work*, Center for Research in Careers, Graduate School of Education, Harvard University, 1967 (unpublished).

Hanson, Pauline, and Carolyn Marmaduke, *The Board Member — decision maker* (Sacramento: Han/Mar Publications [P.O. Box 6143, California 95860]: 1972).

Hirshen, Al, and Vivian Brown, "Public Housing's Neglected Resource: The Tenants," in *City*, published bimonthly by the National Urban Coalition, Fall 1972, pp. 15-21.

Hobman, David, *Who Cares? A Guide to Voluntary and Full-time Social Work* (London & Oxford: Mowbrays, 1971).

Horner, Matina, "Femininity and Successful Achievement: A Basic Inconsistency," in *Feminine Personality and Conflict,* edited by Judith M. Bardwick, Elizabeth Douvan, Matina S. Horner, and David Gutmann (Belmont, California: Brook/Cole Publishing Co., 1970), p. 46.

Hubbell, Hulda, "What Educators Should Know about Volunteering," in *Women's Education,* Vol. 6, No. 1, March 1967, p. 7.

James, Edward T., Janet Wilson, and Paul S. Boyer, *Notable American Women, 1607-1950, A Biographical Dictionary* (Cambridge: Harvard University Press, Belknap Press, 1972).

Johnston, Denis F., "The Future of Work: Three Possible Alternatives," in *Monthly Labor Review,* May 1972, p. 3.

Keller, Suzanne, "Looking Ahead in the 1970's," paper presented at the Radcliffe Institute for a conference on "Women: Resource for a Changing World," April 1972.

Kitzmiller, Michael, and Richard Ottinger, *Citizen Action: Vital Force for Change* (Washington, D.C.: Center for a Voluntary Society, 1971).

Knowles, Malcolm S., "Motivation in Voluntarism: Synopsis of a Theory," in *Journal of Voluntary Action Research,* Vol. 1, No. 2, April 1972, p. 27.

Koretsky, Edna, "The School Volunteer Project in Boston," in *Educational Manpower,* edited by James L. Olivers and Edward Buffie (Bloomington: Indiana University Press, 1970), pp. 103-128.

Kuehn, Lucille, "*American Voluntarism: An Anti-History with Anti-Heroines,*" paper presented at the Radcliffe Institute for a conference on "Women: Resource for a Changing World," April 1972.

Lewis, Michael, "A Conspiracy Theory of Poverty," in *Mulch,* Vol. 2, No. 1, Spring 1972, pp. 31-38.

Lopata, Helen Z., "The Functions of Voluntary Associations in an Ethnic Community: 'Polonia,'" in *Contributions to Urban Sociology* (Chicago: University of Chicago Press, 1964).

MacNeil, Anna Louise, "Should Women Volunteer?" in *Radcliffe Quarterly,* December 1972, p.19.

Marshall, Helen, *Dorothea Dix: Forgotten Samaritan* (Chapel Hill: University of North Carolina Press, 1937).

Maslow, Abraham, "A Theory of Human Motivation: The Goals of Work," in *The Future of Work,* edited by Fred Best (Englewood

Cliffs, N.J.: Prentice-Hall, 1973), pp. 17-32.

McClelland, David C., *The Achieving Society* (Princeton: D. Van Nostrand, 1961).

Minnis, Myra S., "Cleavage in Women's Organizations: A Reflection of the Social Structure of a City," in *American Sociological Review*, 18, February 1953.

N O W (National Organization for Women), *Resolution on Volunteerism*, presented at 5th National Conference, held in Los Angeles, September 1971.

———, *Volunteer — Why Not? Analysis and Answers* (Chicago: Task Force on Women and Volunteerism, 1973).

———, *Volunteerism — What It's All About* (Berkeley: Women and Volunteerism Task Force, 1973).

Copies of all three reports may be obtained from N O W, 1957 E. 73rd Street, Chicago, Ill. 60649

Parker, Stanley, *The Future of Work and Leisure* (New York: Praeger Publishers, Inc., 1972).

Pereira, Joyce E., *A History of Volunteers in Social Welfare in the United States*, Washington, D.C., Catholic University, June 1947 (unpublished thesis).

Poor, Riva, *Four Days, Forty Hours, Reporting a Revolution in Work and Leisure* (Cambridge: Bursk & Poor Publishing, 1970).

Reichert, Irving F., "The Magistrates' Courts: Lay Cornerstone of English Justice," in *Judicature*, Vol. 57, No. 4, November 1973, pp. 138-143.

Schindler, Rainman, and Ronald Lippitt, *The Volunteer Community: Creative Use of Human Resources* (Washington, D.C.: Center for a Voluntary Society, 1971).

Sieder, Violet M., "The Citizen Volunteer in Historical Perspective," in *Perspectives on the American Community* (Chicago: Rand McNally & Co., 1966).

Sills, David L., "Voluntary Associations: Sociological Aspects," in *International Encyclopedia of the Social Sciences*, Vol. 16 (New York: Macmillan and Free Press, 1968).

Simey, Margaret B., *Charitable Effort in Liverpool in the Nineteenth Century* (Liverpool: University Press Liverpool, 1951).

Smith, Bradford, *A Dangerous Freedom* (Philadelphia and New York: J.P. Lippincott Co., 1952, 1954).

Smith, David Horton, "Future Trends in Voluntary Action," in *International Associations*, No. 3, 1972 (reprints available from Center for a Voluntary Society, Washington, D.C.).

———, *Research and Communication Needs in Voluntary Action Evaluat-*

ing Voluntary Action, Occasional Papers No. 2 and No. 3 (Washington D.C.: Center for a Voluntary Society, 1972).

————,"Voluntary Action and Social Problems" *Journal of Voluntary Action Research*, Monograph No. 2, 1971.

————,and John Dixon, *The Voluntary Society* (New York and London: The Free Press, Collier-Macmillan Publishers, 1972).

————,and Richard D. Reddy, *Improving Participation in Voluntary Action* (Washington D.C.: Center for a Voluntary Society, 1971).

————, et al., eds., *Voluntary Action Research*, 1972 and 1973, 2 volumes, (Lexington, Mass.: D.C. Heath & Co., Lexington Books, 1972, 1973).

Spencer, Janet, "Help Wanted — Salary Zero; The Commitment of Political Volunteering," in *Creative Living* (Northwestern Mutual Life, October/November 1972), pp. 1-3.

Spiegel, Hans B. C., "Citizen Participation in Federal Programs: A Review," in *Journal of Voluntary Action Research*, Monograph No. 1, 1971.

Straus, Ellen S., ed., *Call for Action: A Survival Kit for New Yorkers* (New York: Quadrangle Books Inc., 1972).

————,"Equal Work for Unequal Pay," in *Harper's Bazaar*, July 1972, p. 76.

————,"Is It Time for Volunteers' Lib?" in *House and Garden Magazine*, July 1972, pp. 24, 109-114.

————, *The Volunteer Professional, What You Need to Know* (New York: Straus Communications, Inc., on behalf of WMCA: Call for Action, 1972).

Terkel, Studs, *Working: People Talk About What They Do All Day and How They Feel About What They Do* (New York: Pantheon Books, Random House, 1972, 1974).

Toffler, Alvin, *Future Shock* (New York: Bantam Books, by arrangement with Random House, 1970).

Tocqueville, Alexis de, *Democracy in America* (New York: Vintage Books, 1955).

Tresemer, David, and Joseph Pleck, *Maintaining and Changing Sex-Role Boundaries in Men (and Women)*, paper presented at the Radcliffe Institute for a conference on "Women: Resource for a Changing World," April 1972.

Veblen, Thorstein, *The Theory of the Leisure Class* (Boston: Houghton Mifflin, 1972), first published in 1899.

Voluntarism and America's Future, a conference report (Washington, D.C.: Center for a Voluntary Society, February 1972).

The Volunteer Board Member in Philanthropy, Some of His Respon-

sibilities, Achievements and Special Problems (New York: National Information Bureau Inc., 305 E. 45th St., 1968).

Weber, Max, *Politics as a Vocation* (Philadelphia: Fortress Press, 1965).

————,*Protestant Ethic and the Spirit of Capitalism* (New York: Charles Scribner's Sons, 1930).

Weiss, Robert S., and Martin Rein, "The Evaluation of Broad-Aim Programs: Experimental Design, Its Difficulties and an Alternative," in *Administrative Science Quarterly*, Vol. 15, No. 1, March 1970, pp. 97-108.

————,Edwin Harwood, and David Riesman, "Work and Automation: Problems and Prospects," in *Contemporary Social Problems*, edited by Robert K. Merton and Robert Nisbet (New York: Harcourt Brace Jovanovich, Inc., 1971), pp. 545-600.

Work in America, Report of a Special Task Force to the Secretary of Health, Education, and Welfare (Cambridge: The MIT Press, 1973).

Yancey, Theresa, et al., *Recruiting Minority Group and Low Income People as Court Volunteers* (Boulder, Colorado: The National Information Center on Volunteers in Courts, 1971).

Part Two

Abrahams, Ruby B., "Meeting the Needs of the Widowed in a Metropolitan Area," in *Social Work*, September 1972.

————, *Mutual Helping: Styles of Caregiving in a Mutual Help Program* (Boston: Laboratory of Community Psychiatry, Harvard Medical School, 1971).

Bardwick, Judith M., *Psychology of Women, A Study of Bio-Cultural Conflicts* (New York, Evanston, San Francisco, London: Harper & Row, Publishers, 1971).

Bernard, Jessie, "Women and Marriage," paper presented at the Radcliffe Institute for a conference on "Women: Resource for a Changing World," April 1972.

Daniels, Arlene Kaplan, *Volunteerism in the Lives of Women* (San Francisco: Center for the Study of Women in Society [work in progress, due Fall 1974]).

De Rham, Edith, *The Love Fraud: A Direct Attack on the Staggering Waste of Education and Talent Among American Women* (New York: Pegasus, 1965).

Giele, Janet Zollinger, "Women's Strength: An Affirmation," paper presented at the Radcliffe Institute for a conference on "Women: Resource for a Changing World," April 1972.

Ginn, Robert J., *New Directions: A Guide to Opportunities in the Area of*

Social Change and Other Vocational Alternatives (Cambridge: The Office for Graduate and Career Planning, Harvard University, 1970).

Ginsberg, Eli, et al., *Life Styles of Educated Women* (New York: Columbia University Press, 1966).

Goldman, Freda H., *A Turning to Take Next: Alternative Goals in the Education of Women* (Boston: Center for the Study of Liberal Education for Adults, Boston University, July 1970). Copies available free from the Cooperative Extension Service, University of Massachusetts.

Goodman, Ellen, "It isn't easy to just let go," in *Boston Globe*, January 25, 1972.

Gorer, Geoffrey, *Death, Grief, and Mourning* (Garden City: Doubleday and Company, an Anchor Book, 1967).

Corney, Sondra, and Claire Cox, *How Women Can Achieve Fulfillment After Forty* (New York: The Dial Press, 1973).

Gray, Betty Macmorran, "The 'Disuse' of Women, Economics of Sex Bias," in *The Nation*, Vol. 212, No. 24, June 14, 1971, pp. 742-44.

Holmstrom, Lynda Lytle, *The Two Career Family* (Cambridge: Schenkman Publishing Co., 1972).

Janeway, Elizabeth, "Breaking the Age Barrier," in *Ms. Magazine*, April 1973, pp. 50-53, 109-111.

———, *Man's World, Woman's Place: A Study in Social Mythology* (New York: William Morrow and Co., Inc., 1971).

———,"The Weak Are the Second Sex," in *Atlantic Monthly*, December 1973, pp. 91-104.

Johnson, Keith, "Foster Grandparents for Emotionally Disturbed Children," in *Children*, March/April 1967.

Kahne, Hilda, "Women in the Professions," in *Journal of College Placement*, April/May 1973, pp. 59-63.

Krantzler, Mel, *Creative Divorce* (Philadelphia: Evans Lippincott, 1973).

Leisure Guide to Independent Living, an AIM publication (Washington, D.C.: Action for Independent Maturity, American Association for Retired Persons, 1972). Copies available from AIM-AARP, 1225 Connecticut Avenue, N.W., Washington, D.C.

Lindemann, Eric, "Symptomology and Management of Acute Grief," in *Death and Identity*, edited by Robert Fulton (New York: John Wiley, 1965).

Lopata, Helena Z., *Occupation Housewife* (New York: Oxford University Press, 1971).

———*Widowhood in an American City* (Cambridge: Schenkmann Publishing Co., 1972).

Mason, Edward A., *Widows*, a 43-minute, 16-mm documentary film (Boston: Laboratory of Community Psychiatry, Harvard Medical School, 1971). Available for rental.

Mannes, Marya, *They* (Garden City, N.Y.: Doubleday and Co., Inc., 1968).

Matthews, James W., and John F. Thompson, "When People Move . . . " in *Journal of Extension*, University of Wisconsin, Vol. X, No. 2, Summer 1972, pp. 29-35.

Mead, Margaret, "A Next Step in Being a Woman," in *Redbook*, August 1973.

————, *Male and Female* (New York: William Morrow & Co., 1949).

Morris, Robert, Camille Lambert, Jr., and Mildred Guberman, "New Roles for the Elderly, a Study on the Use of the Elderly as Volunteers," in *Papers in Social Welfare, No.10*, edited by Florence Heller, Graduate School for Advanced Studies in Social Welfare, Brandeis University, June 1964.

National Student Volunteer Program, *Directory of College Student Volunteer Programs, Academic Year 1971/2 and 1972/3* (Washington, D.C.: ACTION). Available from Superintendent of Documents, U.S. Government Printing Office.

————, *High School Student Volunteers* (Washington D.C.: ACTION, 1972). Available from Superintendent of Documents, U.S. Government Printing Office.

————,*Synergist*, published three times a year; see "Special High School Issue," Fall 1973 (Washington D.C.: ACTION). Available from Superintendent of Documents, U.S. Government Printing Office.

O'Brien, Patricia, *The Woman Alone* (New York: Quadrangle, The New York Times Book Co., 1973).

Palme, Olof, "The Emancipation of Man," in *Social Issues*, Vol. 28, No. 2, 1972.

Rapoport, Rhoma and Robert N., *Dual-Career Families* (London: Penguin Books, 1971).

Rosenblatt, Aaron, "Interest of Older Persons in Volunteer Activities," in *Social Work*, 11, July 1966.

Rosenthal, Douglas E., Robert Kagan, and Debra Quatrone, *Volunteer Attorneys and Legal Services for the Poor: New York's CLO Program* (New York: Russell Sage Foundation, 1971).

Ruina, Edith, *Moving: A Common-Sense Guide to Relocating Your Family* (New York: Funk and Wagnalls, 1970).

Self, Gerald, *Women on the Move: Some Common Psychological Problems*

(Las Vegas, Nevada, report presented to the Governor's Commission on the Status of Women, June 1969).

Sheresky, Norman, and Marya Mannes, *Uncoupling: The Art of Coming Apart, A Guide to Sane Divorce* (New York: Viking Press, 1972).

Silverman, Phyllis Rolfe, "The Widow to Widow Program," in *Mental Hygiene*, Vol.53, No. 3, July 1969, pp. 333-337.

————,"Factors Involved in Accepting an Offer of Help," in *Archives of the Foundation of Thanatology*, Vol.3, Fall 1971, pp. 161-171.

————,"Services to the Widowed: First Steps in a Program of Preventive Intervention," in *Community Mental Health Journal*, Vol.3, No.1, Spring 1967, pp. 37-44.

————,"Widowhood and Preventive Intervention," in *The Family Coordinator*, January 1972, pp. 95-102 (See its extensive bibliography).

————,"The Widow as a Caregiver in a Program of Preventive Intervention with Other Widows," in *Mental Hygiene*, Vol. 54, No. 4, October 1970, pp. 540-547.

————,"The Funeral Director's Wife as Caregiver," in *Omega*, Vol.2, 1971, pp. 174-178.

————,"How you can help the Newly Widowed," in *Magazine of the American Funeral Director*, May 1970.

————,*Services for the Widowed During the Period of Bereavement* (Boston: Laboratory of Community Psychiatry, Harvard Medical School, 1970).

Simon, Anne W., *The New Years: A New Middle Age* (New York, Alfred A. Knopf, 1968).

Spence, Ann Bennet, and Robert J. Ginn, *Harvard-Radcliffe, Class of 1972* (Cambridge: The Office for Graduate and Career Plans, Harvard University, December 1972).

Summer Opportunities for Young People (Boston: Parents League of Greater Boston, 1972 and 1973). Available from Parents League of Greater Boston, 57 Eliot Street, Jamaica Plain, Boston, Massachusetts 02130.

Start, Clarissa, *When You're a Widow* (St. Louis, Missouri, and London: Concordia Publishing House, 1968).

Tartakoff, Helen H., "Psychoanalytic Perspectives on Women: Past, Present, and Future," paper presented at the Radcliffe Institute for a conference on "Women: Resource for a Changing World," April 1972.

Taves, Isabella, *Women Alone* (New York: Funk and Wagnalls, 1968).

Warner, Alice Sizer, "Voluntarism and Librarianship," in *Library Journal*, April 1, 1972, pp. 1241-1245.

Weiss, Robert S., *The Contributions of an Organization of Single Parents to the Well-Being of Its Members* (Boston: Laboratory of Community Psychiatry, Harvard Medical School, 1971).

———,*Marriage and Alternatives* (Boston: Laboratory of Community Psychiatry, Harvard Medical School, 1972).

———,*Marriage and Other Cross-Sex Relationships* (Boston: Laboratory of Community Psychiatry, Harvard Medical School, 1972).

Wheeler, Michael, *No Fault Divorce* (Boston: Beacon Press 1974).

The Woman in America, edited by Robert Jay Lifton et al. (Boston: Beacon Press, 1967).

Women's Bureau, U.S. Department of Labor, *Facts About Women Heads of Households and Heads of Families* (Washington, D.C.: 1972).

———,*Report of the President's Commission on the Status of Women* (Washington, D.C.: October 1963).

———,*Report on Four Consultations Including: New Patterns in Volunteer Work* (Washington, D.C.: October 1963).

———,*1969 Handbook on Women Workers* (Washington, D.C.: 1969).

———,*Underutilization of Women Workers* (Washington, D.C.: 1971).

Women's Work, a bimonthly magazine published by WOW (Wider Opportunities for Women). Copies and subscription available from WOW, 1111 Twentieth Street, N.W., Washington, D.C. 20036.

Woodhouse, Chase Going, *American Women: The Changing Image* (Boston: Beacon Press, 1963).

Worthington, Gladys, "Older Persons as Community Service Volunteers," in *Social Work* 8, October 1963.

Zuckerman, Eleanor Levine, "The Seven Ages of Woman," in *Radcliffe Quarterly,* March 1973, p. 15.

Part Three and Appendixes

American Friends Service Committee, *Working Loose* (San Francisco: New Vocations Project).

Bolles, Richard Nelson, *What Color Is Your Parachute? A Practical Manual for Job Hunters and Career Changers* (Berkeley: Ten Speed Press, 1972, 1973).

Catalyst Publications, *Self-Guidance Series: G.1 — Planning for Work, G.2 — Your Job Campaign; Education Opportunities Series; Career Opportunities Series* (New York: Catalyst, 1973).

Directory of Counseling Services (Washington, D.C.: International Association of Counseling Services, Inc., 1607 New Hampshire Avenue, N.W.).

Friedman, Sande, and Lois C. Schwartz, *No Experience Necessary: A Guide to Employment for the Female Liberal Arts Graduate* (New

York: Dell Publishing Co., 1971).

Ginzberg, Eli, *Career Guidance: Who Needs It, Who Provides It, Who Can Improve It?* (New York: McGraw-Hill, 1971).

Huth, Carol Monnik, ed., *Return Engagement: A Woman's Guide to Part-Time Work and Study in Philadelphia* (Bryn Mawr: Bryn Mawr College, 1970 — published jointly by the alumnae associations of Barnard, Bryn Mawr, Mount Holyoke, Radcliffe, Smith, Vassar, Wellesley, and the University of Pennsylvania, Program for the Continuing Education of Women).

Invest Yourself: A Catalogue of Service Opportunities, edited by James Neal Cavener and published annually by The Commission on Voluntary Service and Action, 475 Riverside Drive, New York, N.Y. 10027, from which it may be ordered.

King, Alice Gore, *Help Wanted — Female: The Young Woman's Guide to Job Hunting* (New York: Charles Scribner's Sons, 1968).

The New York Times Guide to Continuing Education in America (New York: Quadrangle Books, 1973).

An Operating Manual for a Volunteer Talent Pool, edited by Janet Burgoon and Joan Winter, Winnetka, Ill., January 1967.

Oppenheimer, Valerie Kincade, "Occupational Opportunities for Women," paper presented at the Radcliffe Institute for a conference on "Women: Resource for a Changing World," April 1972.

Prentice, Barbara A., *The Back to Work Handbook for Housewives* (New York: Macmillan Company, Collier Books, 1971).

Report of the Conference on Human Needs and Voluntary Service, sponsored by the Alumnae Association of Smith College at Northampton, Massachusetts, January 9-19, 1973.

Resources for Action: A Voluntarism Resource Directory, edited by Lydia V. Cerullo (Washington, D.C., and Boston: Center for a Voluntary Society, Fall 1974).

Schwartz, Felice N., Margaret Schifter, and Susan S. Gillotti, *How to Go to Work When Your Husband Is Against It, Your Children Aren't Old Enough, and There's Nothing You Can Do Anyhow*, A Catalyst Publication (New York: Simon and Schuster, 1972).

Schwartz, Jane, *Part-Time Employment: Employer Attitudes on Opportunities for the College-Trained Woman*, report of a pilot project (New York: Alumnae Advisory Center [54 Madison Avenue], 1964).

Scobey, Joan, and Lee Parr McGrath, *Creative Careers for Women: A Handbook of Sources and Ideas for Part-Time Jobs* (New York: Simon and Schuster, 1968).

Scofield, Nanette E., and Betty Klarman, *So You Want to Go Back to*

Work! For the Woman Interested in a New and Satisfying Second Career (New York: Random House, 1968).

Second Careers for Women: A View from the San Francisco Peninsula, report of a conference on Second Careers for Women, held at Stanford, California, May 2, 1970, edited by Jane D. Fairbank and Susan Groag Bell.

Swanson, Mary T., *Your Volunteer Program: Organization and Administration of Volunteer Programs* (Ankeny, Iowa: EPDA Volunteer Coordinators Program, Des Moines Area Community College, April 1972).

U.S. Department of Labor, *Continuing Education Programs and Services for Women* (Washington, D.C.: Government Printing Office).

————,Bureau of Labor Statistics, *Occupational Outlook Handbook,* Bulletin 185 (Washington, D.C.: Government Printing Office).

————,Women's Bureau, *Careers for Women in the Seventies* (Washington, D.C.: Government Printing Office, 1972).

————,*Continuing Education Programs and Services for Women* (Washington, D.C.: Government Printing Office, 1971).

Vocations for Social Change, *People's Yellow Pages* (Cambridge, 1973).

Washington Opportunities for Women: A Guide to Part-Time Work and Study for the Educated Woman, edited by Reyna Weisl, Jane Fleming, and Mary Janney (Washington, D.C.: Robert B. Luce, Inc., 1967).

White, Martha S., ed., *The Next Step: A Guide to Part-Time Opportunities in Greater Boston for the Educated Woman* (Cambridge: Radcliffe Institute for Independent Study, 1964).

Women's Yellow Pages, edited by Carol Freedman Edry and Ginnie Goulet, 1st edition (Cambridge: Boston Women's Collective, 1972), and 2d edition (Boston: Boston Women's Collective, 1974).

Index

251